Seasons of the Sea

Seasons of the Sea

BY Monique Corriveau

ABRIDGED AND TRANSLATED BY

David Homel

ILLUSTRATED BY

Debi Perna

A Groundwood Book
Douglas & McIntyre
TORONTO/VANCOUVER

This present edition is an adaptation and abridgement of the original work, *Les saisons de la mer,* by Monique Corriveau.

Groundwood Books/Douglas & McIntyre Ltd.
26 Lennox Street, 3rd Floor
Toronto, Ontario M6G 1J4

Canadian Cataloguing in Publication Data

Corriveau, Monique, 1930-1976
[Les saisons de la mer. English]
Seasons of the sea

Translation of: Les saisons de la mer.
ISBN 0-88899-086-3

I. Title. II. Title: Les saisons de la mer.
English.

PS8505.077S3313 1989 jC843'.54 C89-093414-2
P27.C677Se 1989

Book design by Michael Solomon
Illustrations by Debi Perna
Printed and bound in Canada

1 2 3 4 5 6 7 8 9 6 5 4 3 2 1 0 9 8

To Suzanne Duff and
Isabelle Corriveau,
two little girls
the same age.

This is almost a true story, the tale of the real Mary Lou, who grew up on Oderin, a little island in Placentia Bay, in Newfoundland, in the years around 1910. Helena Frecker was kind enough to let me use the memoires that she had written down for her own children.

Tonight, there is a restlessness in the wind
And a small rain that has salt in it from the sea,
And the white breakers wander in the dark.
Way down in the west the waning moon calls to the sea
Sweeping back the flood from the black points of land
And the tide is turning from the seven rocks.

—Traditional song from the Hebrides Islands

CHAPTER ONE

The Four-Legged Schoolboy

MARY LOU MCGUIRE WATCHED THE SEA FROM her schoolhouse window. The North Atlantic seemed to be breathing, trying to break free from its ice prison. This year, storms had been breaking over Newfoundland one after the other, and in the evenings, fishermen talked things over by their firesides. Winter had driven them back to their homes.

Wind swept over the little island of Oderin, howling as it shook the schoolhouse that clung to the rock. The teacher rang the bell, and the students poured into the one-room schoolhouse. Twenty in all, they settled in at their desks with a great commotion, boys on the right, girls on the left. Everyone was bundled up; it was just as cold inside as out.

Tom Griffith, the oldest student, lit a fire in the wood stove, and snowy boots were set around it. Inkwells slowly thawed. In an hour's time, the students would be able to write with ink instead of on slates.

Mary Lou whispered to Brigitte Jarvis, her best friend. They laughed and schemed together. There were many secrets to share right before Christmas.

Suddenly a whisper ran through the class. A big black dog was pressing his nose against the window. It was Pierrot, Mary Lou's Newfoundland retriever. He always found her, no matter where she went. Mr. Burke, the teacher, used to say that if only all his students were as zealous as this four-legged schoolboy, Oderin would produce the world's greatest minds.

The door began to tremble, as though a wild wind were beating it. Suddenly it gave way and swung open. But it wasn't the wind that came bursting into the classroom; it was the huge dog with his fur sticking up every which way. The dog shook himself, scattering snow everywhere, knocked over the benches, gave friendly licks to everyone in sight and spilled the inkwells, sending blue streams rushing across the floor.

Two of the youngest pupils jumped up on the teacher's desk, and a third whimpered from behind the wood stove. Mr. Burke should have been furious, but he looked resigned and called for quiet.

Tom Griffith grabbed hold of Pierrot's collar and tried to drag him towards the door and the freezing December air. But he was not strong enough to budge the dog. Then Mary Lou put her arm around the dog's neck and whispered a few words in his ear.

"Come on, Pierrot, wait for me outside," she said in French. And Pierrot quietly walked out the door.

"Quiet now, children!" Mr. Burke shut the door. His voice was solemn and a little husky.

Everyone sat up straight and attentive. A writing slate fell with a sharp crack, but no one heard it. Mary Lou was all ears.

"In January," Mr. Burke said, "I won't be coming back. The government has to close the school because there is no more money."

At first his words were greeted with surprise and consternation. Then the students began to picture the freedom: no more lessons, no more punishments after class, no being forced to sit still on these rock-hard benches. There would be no more teacher for Oderin.

"Thank you, sir. Merry Christmas!" the children cried and fled from the school like seagulls on the wing.

Brigitte drew her little flock of brothers and sisters around her like a shepherdess.

"Merry Christmas, Mary Lou!" she called out.

Like an echo, her little brothers and sisters repeated, "Merry Christmas, Merry Christmas, Mary Lou!"

Mary Lou lingered on the schoolhouse steps. One last time, her eyes wandered over the nearly empty room, then came to rest on the calendar.

Tom was arranging the benches. "Nobody will be tearing off the pages anymore," he said. "Do you want this last one?"

She slipped the piece of paper between the pages of a book. The last class in Oderin: December 24th, 1912.

"Thank you, Tom."

"I'll carry your books. We're both going the same way."

Pierrot reappeared. He ran around them, bounding here and there, disappearing only to return in a great cloud of powdery snow. Heads down, they walked along in comfortable silence.

The road ran above the sea. Shunted along by the currents, masses of ice came together with an immense crash. The constant groan of the ice would always be the sound of winter for Mary Lou. The salty east wind drove along the ocean fog, and with its icy breath, it whipped up the surface of Placentia Bay. It was never very cold in Newfoundland, not as cold as on the mainland of Canada. The sea built up a storehouse of warmth during the summer and sheltered the island from harsh temperatures.

Mary Lou never tired of the landscape and the thousand shades of colour between black and white: the charcoal-grey rocks, the water with its ever-changing opaque quality, hidden in the thick fog, and the snow that changed colours with the light.

Tom looked silently at the moving horizon. *How different he is from David*, Mary Lou thought, picturing her older brother.

Until last year, the two boys had been like two of a kind. But events had separated them. One now went to boarding-school in St. John's, the capital of Newfoundland, and the other had had no choice but to stay in the little school in Oderin. Though he was a year younger, at thirteen, Tom was stronger and more mature than his older friend. People in Oderin said it was high time for Tom to start fishing with his father and take on his share of the family responsibilities.

"David will be back soon," Mary Lou announced, blurting out her big piece of news.

But Tom only said, "Oh."

Mary Lou began to daydream again. The only sounds were their big sailor's boots and the call of the wind and the cracking of ice.

Tom stopped in front of his modest house. "See you later, Mary Lou. And Merry Christmas!"

Mary Lou raced home. At the foot of a hill stood her house, a dwelling that was built as simply as the others, only larger, with a turret and porch. This was Mary Lou's harbour and kingdom. She had known no other home.

She went inside, threw her satchel on the bench, one mitten here, another there, and called at the top of her lungs, "Mum, I'm home!"

"Hello, Mary Lou," her mother answered from the kitchen where she was readying the holiday feast.

From the living room, her father asked, "Do you always have to yell so loud?"

Mary Lou ran over to kiss him. His glasses pushed up on his forehead and his eyes mischievous, he was sitting at the piano, tapping out his favourite tune with two fingers, for he had never taken lessons. Once he had found the notes he was looking for, he sang along with the piano. The song sounded sad, especially the Irish words. Mary Lou plunked herself down next to him on the piano bench.

"Papa, Mr. Burke is leaving. We won't have to go to school anymore."

"I know," said Mr. McGuire, his face growing dark. "It's a shame for Oderin's children."

"I'm sure they're delighted," Anne put in.

Mary Lou's older sister descended the stairs majestically. A wet towel around her neck was designed to cure her sore throat. Anne was forced to stay inside with a cold, which spoiled her greatest pleasure. At thirteen, she was extremely fond of school, probably because she was the top student.

"Hmmm, something smells good." Mary Lou sniffed the air.

"Mum and Sarah are making apple turnovers for David," Anne said.

"For David and the rest of us," added Mr. McGuire, who loved apple turnovers himself.

CHAPTER TWO

Hello, David!

DAVID MCGUIRE LEANED ON THE RAILING. THE *Glencoe* danced over the waves and the ice seemed to spin in slow-motion, making the passengers dizzy.

David watched a big block of ice with bluish flanks strike the hull, then slip past the ship.

Oderin, with its steep rocks, its houses scattered in the hollows of its bays, and the little church with its neighbouring school, loomed up out of the fog. He had left two months ago, and he never thought he would be so happy to see it again.

Early in the nineteenth century, the village had been an important place. Countless boats dropped anchor on a regular basis, and the fisheries employed up to one hundred and fifty workers. But times had changed. Now Oderin was no more than a little fishing port on Placentia Bay, off Argentia. It was all the *Glencoe* could do to stop off there every ten days, facing wind and tides to carry provisions and news from island to island.

David had chatted with the captain, a friend of his father's. There was no one on the Placentia coast who did not know Phillip McGuire, the magistrate and only merchant on the island of Oderin.

Of all the family, David had missed Mary Lou the most. There she was at the end of the wharf, jumping up and down, waving a red scarf. Pierrot was with her, of course, and everyone on Oderin seemed to be crowded around them.

The boat prepared for docking. Little clouds rose up from people's mouths. In the cold air, the steam from the blackened chimney seemed to breathe, too, as it sounded its triumphant siren.

"Here I am," it seemed to announce, "with my vigilant crew, my joyful passengers and the mail bursting with Christmas gifts for all of you. Here I am, with my cargo of happiness."

The call of the captain's voice was heard over the howling wind and the groaning motors. The *Glencoe* struck the wharf, the ropes were tied amid a great straining and creaking, and the gangway was thrown down. David was the first one off.

Amazed, Mary Lou took a long look at her brother. Was this really David, this strapping young man with the serious look? His thin face had grown longer. He was nothing like the carefree boy who had set out two months ago for St. John's. How could she ever play with this grown-up?

He bent over and brushed his little sister's round cheeks with his lips. Was that a moustache scratching her? He picked her up for a closer look.

"You've shrunk!" he said. Then his voice gave out on him and he made a terrible croaking noise.

"You're the one who's changed," Mary Lou shot back, recovering her poise. "You smell like tobacco."

"Shhh," he cautioned her.

David smoked now, and he had no intention of broadcasting the fact. Like Pierrot, Mary Lou had long since learned to trust her nose when it came to judging people and things, and not just depend on her eyes and ears. Oderin's children were fragrant with herbs and seaweed

Of all the family, David had missed Mary Lou the most.

during the summer. In winter, there was the constant smell of smoke from the schoolhouse stove. Brigitte's little sister gave off the sweet scent of the wild hyacinth she picked on the headlands during the summer. And her sister Anne cheated with that tiny perfume bottle she had ordered from the French island of Saint Pierre.

Now the whole family crowded around David. Even Mr. McGuire had to look up at him.

CHAPTER THREE
An Accident

"HEY, PAPA! HEY, MUM!"

Mary Lou ran through the house, searching for her parents.

She stopped in the office doorway and, for a moment, watched her parents without them knowing. They were reading quietly, absorbed in their thoughts. There was a kind of happiness in the room, and as they exchanged a quick glance, Mary Lou realized something she had never known before. Her parents were separate from her, with a life of their own away from her or David, Anne or Jerome.

Father was sitting in his favourite armchair by the fire. He was ten days behind the rest of the world, and when the *Glencoe* came in, he hurried to catch up by reading the daily papers in chronological order.

Her face flushed and her eyes shining, a few strands of hair falling from her bun, Mrs. McGuire had hustled through the holiday preparations. Now she was taking time to sit down, and she glanced through the most recent paper. Soon she would have to go back to her work and help Sarah, the cook, in the kitchen.

"Hey, Papa and Mum!"

They looked up at Mary Lou with a smile.

"Can I go out and play?"

"Go ahead, Mary Lou," her mother answered. "Anne will help me."

Mary Lou went out to join her friends. She looked for Pierrot, but he was nowhere to be found. The dog had been driven to distraction by the delicious cooking smells, and was banished from the house. He must have decided to disappear.

Just as well, Mary Lou told herself. The smaller kids are afraid of him.

She ran happily down the hill that overlooked the wild, frozen sea. Her friends called out, yelling at her to hurry. Brigitte was there with her collection of younger brothers.

Mary Lou pulled her sled up the steep slope. Voices rang out in the cold air. The children stamped their feet as they waited their turn to slide and blew on their fingers and curled them up inside their mittens.

The slope had hardened, and the children sped down faster and faster, the wind slapping their burning cheeks. Night was falling as they climbed back up the hill one more time, dead tired, but drunk with speed and pleasure. What if a sled flew over the edge and went plunging into the sea . . . no use thinking about it. They stopped just in time and their hearts skipped a beat, then they laughed all the harder.

Mary Lou's sled hardly touched the ground. It bounded from one rough spot to the next and overturned a short distance farther on. Her eyes filled with tears. There was snow down her back, and Mary Lou wished the moment would last forever.

Tired and frozen stiff, the children gathered on the shore. They did not have the strength to climb the hill one more time. Their limbs were heavy with fatigue, and they shivered under the wind, but they did not want to say goodbye.

But it was time to go home. After the evening meal, Christmas Eve would begin.

The older children stayed behind to chat, while the younger ones ventured out towards the sea, where the floating ice formed a treacherous, moving platform on the edge of the shore. Farther out the ocean was too deep and salty to freeze.

Soon the whole careless lot of them were running across the ice, jumping on the slippery crust, calculating the distances, losing their balance, righting themselves, laughing at their own fear. It was against the rules, but their parents would never know.

This was Mary Lou's favourite sport, and she went at it with great abandon. Normally, Anne or David made her be careful, but they were nowhere in sight, and she could play to her heart's content. She had a good pair of legs, a good eye, and she was not in danger.

Little by little, she moved away from the others. Despite her better judgement, she was tempted by the awesome spectacle of the moving ice, by the deep voice of the colliding blocks. She realized Pierrot would have never let her go this far. He would have held her back by the edge of her coat. For once, she did not mind that he wasn't there.

But suddenly she had gone too far. The farther she travelled from the shoreline, the more unstable the ice was. It grew thinner and thinner and began to break under her weight.

For a moment, Mary Lou felt as though she were suspended over the void. Then she slipped. She cried out, just before she disappeared under the edge of the ice.

The brutal cold seized her. She struggled to the surface for a moment, but her waterlogged clothing dragged her down again.

Her friends heard her cries. Panicking, they ran back and forth helplessly, afraid to come too close. Stretching out her arms towards them, she swallowed a mouthful of water, coughed, then sank again.

This was Mary Lou's favourite sport, and she went at it with great abandon.

A few minutes earlier, David had left the house, armed with an axe to cut down the Christmas tree for the living-room. As he walked towards the nearby woods, he noticed strange movements on the beach.

David could barely make out what was happening in the darkness, but he did not waste any time. He ran towards the sea, faster and faster as he came down the hill. He leaped across crevasses and over heaps of stones. Twice he fell to his knees, then picked himself up, his eyes still riveted on the white toque he knew only too well. It was Mary Lou's hat.

He ran past the panicky children. He ordered them back to dry land and safety, then moved on through water up to his waist. Suddenly he spotted the white toque among the broken pieces of ice. He reached over and with one hand grabbed Mary Lou's coat, then pulled her from the water and cradled her in his arms.

"Don't be afraid, Mary Lou. Don't be afraid. It's all over now."

Soaked to the skin, he climbed out of the water. Despite his load, he ran towards the house and its lighted windows.

Inside, he called for help. His father's strong arms took Mary Lou. Shaken, Mr. McGuire carried her upstairs to the girls' room, where her mother changed her into dry clothes and wrapped her in a heavy sweater and blankets.

"Could I have the birch log?" Mary Lou asked in a wavering voice.

The log was a big piece of wood kept in the stove and used as a foot-warmer. The two sisters often asked for it on winter evenings, and now Mary Lou eased her feet onto its shiny surface. The gentle heat comforted her. She sipped a strong cup of tea and sneezed, as her sister predicted that she would catch cold tomorrow.

Pierrot dashed in, as though he had come to ask forgiveness for not having been there. *If I'd stayed with Mary Lou*, he seemed to say, *nothing would have happened*.

Mary Lou yawned in his face. Her eyes grew heavy. She fell asleep peacefully, holding her mother's hand.

A few hours later, Mary Lou awoke. A strange sound had interrupted her sleep. The birch log was still giving off its comforting heat.

A joyful noise was coming from downstairs. Curious, she put on her bathrobe and slippers and went down quickly with Pierrot.

She saw an Indian with long feathers and a garish tattoo walking down the hall. Suddenly, she remembered. On Christmas Eve, the villagers, dressed as their ancestors had dressed long ago, visited all the families on the island who would open their doors to them.

Mary Lou squatted on the bottom step so she could look into the kitchen without being seen.

A trapper wearing a mask and a fur hat played the harmonica. The villagers, dressed in their old-fashioned costumes, danced a jig and sang together.

Suddenly the door flew open and a pine tree came walking in. From somewhere behind the branches came David's hoarse voice. Bending under the burden, he asked for help.

The guests sprang to their feet, picked up the trunk and shook the snow from the branches. David straightened up with a laugh as his father came in behind him, carrying the axe.

They stood the tree in one corner of the room to thaw onto some old newspapers. Then the neighbours said that it was a shame, but it was getting time to go.

David wanted to join them on their rounds through the island, but he knew that on Christmas Eve, his father would have been sorry to see him go. So the family went to the door and waved goodbye to their guests. "Merry Christmas," they called out into the night.

Now, there was work to do.

"It's time to decorate the tree," Mr. McGuire declared.

First they fastened the tree to a base made of two planks, then they carried it into the living-room. Mrs. McGuire discovered Mary Lou dozing halfway up the stairs, with her dog as a pillow. They carried her to the sofa and made a nest of blankets for her.

David climbed a step-ladder to put up the star, while Jerome, underfoot, got in everybody's way. Anne attached the tiny candelabras to the branches. They held real candles, in all the colours of the rainbow. Mr. McGuire carefully lit the little flames.

Anne bent over and set out the figures of the Nativity scene. Mr. McGuire had sculpted them when the children were very young.

"It's even prettier than last year," Mary Lou sighed.

Mr. McGuire took out the Bible. On the endpapers were written the names of three generations of McGuires, from their grandfather, the first to come from Ireland to settle on Oderin, to David, Anne, Mary Lou and Jerome. In a glance, the reader could discover the important dates in their lives: the births, marriages and deaths.

As Mary Lou turned the pages, yellowed with time, she wondered what would be written about her life, some day.

CHAPTER FOUR

The Friendly Seal

CHRISTMAS DAY! THROUGH THE GLASS DOORS in the living-room, Mary Lou saw the mysterious packages at the foot of the tree. It was almost eight o'clock. But before anyone could open the presents, they had to go to church.

The priest from Burin, one of the mainland villages, came to Oderin two or three times a year. The other Sundays, the islanders had to come together on their own to pray.

This Christmas, the little run-down church had been given a new face. The long streaks that ran down the wall reminded the faithful that the roof leaked every time it rained. The varnish was chipping off the pews and the broken windowpanes were sealed over with boards. But everything else was clean and shiny. Plants had been set out everywhere.

Despite the damp cold, the men and women of Oderin were glad to be together. As he did every week, Phillip McGuire read the Epistles, then the Gospel. Standing erect, with his glasses pushed up on his forehead – since he only used them for reading – Phillip McGuire recited the rosary in his deep strong voice.

Mary Lou was so proud of him, and glad that everyone on Oderin knew she was Phillip McGuire's daughter. A few minutes later, Tom, the official bell-ringer, grabbed the rope and pulled with all his might. The bells rang madly, and their voices kept time for Mary Lou as she raced along. She dragged her father by the hand, and he laughed even as he protested against such rushed treatment. They both headed for the house, which was all decked out in its holiday finery.

She caught Pierrot by the collar and locked him up in the shed. The dog did not understand why he was being punished, since he had not done anything wrong.

Mary Lou explained to him, "Papa and Mum say you'll start breaking things if you're in the house. I guess they're right. Be good and I'll be back just as soon as I can."

"Come on, we're waiting for you!" the others called out.

In solemn procession, they entered the living-room. There a mystery greeted them. At the foot of the tree was a pile of six packages all alike – six big cubes wrapped in green paper. Papa kept one for himself and gave one to each member of the family.

"Skates!" David cried.

The steel blades shone in the candlelight. The skates had thin supple laces to tie them to the skater's shoes. What a surprise! Everyone had a pair. They would have great games on the frozen pond that sparkled like a mirror at the bottom of the hill.

Mrs. McGuire was a little less enthusiastic. She had not put on a pair of skates since she was a girl. The gift was really a surprise.

The smell of roast chicken floated into the living-room. Sarah had left the kitchen to share in the family celebration, but now she retreated to her kingdom, weighed down with gifts: a sweater, a pair of slippers and Mrs. McGuire's discovery, a spiny cactus. It had travelled a long way to this isolated village, so different from its native desert.

"Let's eat!" Mr. McGuire called out.

The children hurried through the meal because, according to custom, they unwrapped the gifts from St. John's while their parents drank their tea. These presents were called "Uncle Paul's Christmas."

Paul O'Neill, Mrs. McGuire's brother, sent a package every year, several weeks before the holidays. And every year, the parents hid it in their closet. It was an open secret, of course, but this year the bigness of the parcel intrigued everyone more than usual.

Mary Lou was given the honour of opening the package. The string snapped, the heavy paper crackled, and there were the presents, each individually wrapped in pretty coloured paper, the kind you can only find in the city.

David dived in first. He came up with a big book with gold binding: the story of Grenfell's travels, the English doctor who had founded many hospitals in Labrador.

For Mrs. McGuire, there was a soft shawl made of Scottish wool, perfect for winter evenings. There was a practical gift, too. It was a small, heavy packet that gave off all sorts of unusual smells – spices from countries far beyond the seas. Mary Lou read the names that spoke of mysterious lands: cinnamon, ginger, saffron. The spices represented past journeys that had much to do with the history of Newfoundland.

"Like all the explorers," Mr. McGuire explained, "the first Europeans to land in America were seeking the route to the Indies. The spices imported by Arab caravans and sold by Venetian merchants were very, very expensive. The explorers came here to buy them directly. But they found a much more lasting source of wealth: the cod-fisheries."

"Cod's a lot duller, if you ask me," Mary Lou said.

"That's what people in the Indies would say about spices," Anne replied.

Mr. McGuire inspected his gift. It was a mysterious object, a black metal cube full of buttons, complete with a lens. "It's a camera," he told his astonished daughter.

Mary Lou tried to imagine what this complicated-looking machine had to do with the pictures Uncle Paul often sent them, showing her cousins all dressed up in their prettiest outfits.

"Poor girl, you've got a lot to learn. It's time you took a little trip," David said.

"She'll have to go to boarding-school," Anne put in.

Their parents traded glances. Mary Lou did not miss a thing. Some special significance was attached to the word "boarding-school."

Then Mary Lou opened her present. She lifted the cover and found herself staring at a baby seal, who was staring back at her with glass eyes. A *stuffed* baby seal, of course. His fur was thick, rough and woolly, yellowish-white like the wool from the sheep that her friend Brigitte's father raised.

Mary Lou grabbed the seal with both hands, rubbed it against her cheek and buried her face in its bristly fur. The seal would replace her old dolls and be her companion, her confidant, her friend.

"Look at him, Anne, look!"

But Anne was posing in front of the mirror, trying on the pink velvet belt she had received. The belt brought out the grace of her figure and the bloom of her skin. She ran one hand through her thick dark hair and paid no attention to her younger sister.

"Miss McGuire, very pleased to make your acquaintance," she bowed to the mirror.

Mary Lou was appalled. This kind of behaviour was high treason. She slipped up behind Anne and stuck her tongue out at her sister in the mirror. Mary Lou looked so comical with her stuffed seal and her mutinous expression that Anne had to laugh, and Mary Lou ended up blushing.

Meanwhile, her parents were reading Uncle Paul's letter. There was something in their attitude that worried her. "We'll have to make a decision," she heard her father say, before he slipped the letter into his pocket.

That evening, Mary Lou nestled down in the feather bed she shared with her sister. Anne went to bed later, which was fine with Mary Lou, since that gave her the room all to herself.

She talked to her baby seal in a hushed voice. Not that she expected an answer, but she had many secrets to share tonight. She would not tell anyone about her new confidant. At eleven, a girl was much too old for such childish things.

There was a knock at the door. Quickly she pulled the quilt over the seal, which made for a strange-looking lump on the pillow.

"Come in!" she called.

It was David. He offered her a mint candy, then sat down on the foot of her bed. It did not take him long to notice the lump on the pillow.

"That's my seal," she said.

He had no intention of making fun of her.

"Did you know," he said as he examined it, "that they call these animals 'white coats'?"

Mary Lou nodded. David was just like his father. He liked to share his knowledge, and he soon launched into a story. He had never taken part in the seal hunt, of course, but he had heard the Oderin fishermen's stories of their adventurous expeditions.

Towards winter's end, the trawlers went off to challenge the North Atlantic. Using dynamite and towing the boat when there was an ice jam, the men reached the spot where the seals born every February lay on the ice, camouflaged by their white coats. Their parents fed and watched over them as they grew into adults. Once their fur turned black and shiny, they joined the other seals in the ocean.

When a herd of these animals was spotted, the men left the ship and fanned out, leaping across the rolling ice, a moving plain whipped by the waves.

"They sure are brave!" exclaimed Mary Lou, who still had painful memories of her own adventure at sea.

"That's right," David said. "And too bad for those who don't make it back to ship by nightfall, because they freeze to death."

The sad cry of the siren would call for hours, summoning the men back, but some never returned. Other times the trawler drifted off. Crushed to splinters by the ice floes, the boat would sink to the bottom without a trace.

"How do the hunters catch the seals?"

"Every man has a gaff, a long stick with an iron hook at the end. They kill the seals with it, skin them and drag the skins back to the boat."

When David saw Mary Lou's face, he was sorry he had described the hunt.

She whispered stories to him, then stopped to listen to him in the silence that followed.

"Poor Mary Lou, you're as white as a ghost. I shouldn't have told you about it."

"I'll never, never wear a fur coat," she promised.

Once her brother had left, she set her seal on the quilt.

It was almost like an ice floe. She whispered stories to him, then stopped to listen as he spoke to her of the sea, his private world, dark and friendly, inhabited by a thousand creatures she had never seen.

CHAPTER FIVE
The House at the Edge of the World

VACATION WENT BY AS QUICK AS A FLASH.

The next thing David knew, he was taking out his shirts, new ties, socks and everything else a boarding-school student might need and putting them into his trunk. With a heavy heart, he finished packing. His sisters had wanted him to join in their games, and they had not left him much leisure. Walks with his father, visits to people in Oderin, odd jobs that were saved for the oldest son – vacation had turned out to be a very busy time. The iceboat he had started on Boxing Day was not even ready, and that very afternoon he was to board the *Glencoe*.

Back to St. John's . . . while all he could think about was Oderin.

He picked up the book he had not had time to finish, and soon he was reading again, absorbed by the story.

In 1892, Grenfell, a young English doctor, journeyed to Labrador. He had come to treat the inhabitants of the arid coast, which was largely a wintering-over spot for fishing families. For twenty years, he devoted himself to setting up hospitals, schools and cooperatives, there and on the northern coast of Newfoundland.

David considered the doctor's life. He dreamed of devoting himself to helping others, as Grenfell had. But was he up to the task?

He went to think things over in the shed, to the sound of hammer and nails. With a little luck, he could finish his iceboat. Just then Mary Lou showed up. She dreaded her brother's departure and wanted to spend as much time as she could with him.

"Hello, David. What are you doing?"

A grunt was the only answer. He was holding nails in his mouth, the way Sarah did with pins when she was letting out the girls' dresses. He had already built the raft part, and now he was attaching old skate blades to it.

He rose to his feet, triumphant. "Now let's look for a mast."

David chose a strong, straight piece of wood and cut the branches off carefully. Mary Lou held it steady on the raft. With the help of the nails, a T-square and some planks, David attached the mast to the platform. He even found something to cut the sail with.

"Help me take the boat down to the sea."

"But, David, it's too dangerous."

"Don't worry, I know how to drive."

Admiration shone in Mary Lou's eyes. What an ingenious brother she had!

"I'll help you – but on one condition," she said.

"What's that?"

"That you take me with you."

"You? You're just a kid."

"I'll be twelve next fall."

"Great! That's nine months away."

"All right, do it yourself then."

She walked off, waiting for him to call her back. Which is exactly what happened, since David did need her. Pushing and pulling, they towed the vehicle down to the thick, smooth ice in the harbour. The sail swelled and the sled started gathering speed.

"Fabulous!" David called over the voice of the sea.

But Mary Lou was not so sure. The bumps and bangs knocked her head against the mast, which they clung to desperately. Ready for action, his muscles straining, David made the most of the wind to tack about. He held Mary Lou by the shoulder. He knew his sister. Even if she was scared stiff, she would never admit defeat.

Behind the frozen ice-shapes, the sea stretched out forever, merging with the foggy sky. The sled flew over the frozen surface, where heaped-up blocks of ice cast blue shadows. All around the bay stood the rocks, massive, black and shiny.

That brilliant image would always remain in David's memory. Two hours later, he was on a ship leaving Oderin behind, and the island was no more than a tiny point. Looking outward, David gazed at the endless horizon. For him, this was just the first step of a long journey.

That night, sleep would not come to Mary Lou. She could feel her blood rushing through her body. Next to her, Anne was reading. The pages crackled as she turned them.

Outside, the imprisoned waves were invisible, but Mary Lou could hear their icy chains. In St. John's harbour, you could not hear the sea so clearly, not like here. That was what David had said. When he left, he hinted that some day soon, his sisters would be leaving with him.

Anne would be happy at boarding school, with friends

her own age, he had said. But Mary Lou was a different story. It was hard to imagine her living in that fishbowl atmosphere. She would miss the open air on Oderin, just as David did.

Suddenly a window slammed somewhere in the house. She sat up with a start and listened. The noise continued to the rhythm of the gusts of wind.

It was either get up or listen to the window slamming all night. Barefoot on the cold tiles, she ran down the hallway. The noise came from the farthest room, David's room. She went into it, her heart pounding in spite of herself.

Cold air was pouring into the room. In the moonlight, something moved. Was it a ghost, like in one of Sarah's stories? No. Just a jacket, hanging from a chair.

She had not stopped to light a lamp, and now she wished she had. In the shadows, she recognized an open book: *The Travels of Doctor Grenfell*. David must have forgotten it there. She thought that at that very moment, on board the *Glencoe* to Placentia, or perhaps in the St. John's train, David was thinking of her, too. Suddenly it was as if David was there in the darkness before her.

She heard a low voice, steps on the stairway. Someone must have heard her from downstairs. Mary Lou knew from the quick step that it was her father. He halted in the doorway, candle in hand, and listened.

"It's me, Papa," Mary Lou whispered.

"Do you miss David? I'm sure he's thinking of us, too."

He came closer and put the candle-holder on the table. Pools of light danced, then settled. The darkness was still thick but it was not threatening anymore, as her father took her back to her room.

But even as his daughter slept, Mr. McGuire was not at peace. David's departure had rekindled his concern. Would his children leave him, one by one, now that the school was but an empty shell? Mr. McGuire imagined his family scattered to the four winds. Had he laboured all his life for that? Was there no other way?

CHAPTER SIX
Bread Day

"YOU CAN'T HEAR YOURSELF THINK WHEN SARah's baking bread," Mrs. McGuire said.

The cook's vibrant, lusty voice sent Irish echoes rolling through the house.

"Are you writing Papa a letter?" Mary Lou asked. "Isn't he coming from Saint Pierre and Miquelon today?"

"He is. But it's good to write what's on your mind when you're thinking of someone."

Mary Lou knew what her mother meant. She wrote David things she would never dare say out loud. On paper, it was easy for her to put down her thoughts.

But there was more there than met the eye. Mrs. McGuire had never looked so distracted, so care-worn as during the last ten days, ever since the *Glencoe* had brought her a certain letter that she must have read a good hundred times. Mary Lou suspected something was afoot. The night before, she had broached the subject with her sister. Anne had not noticed anything out of the ordinary, but she promised to keep her ears and eyes open.

She never sees anything anyway, Mary Lou thought with a trace of bitterness.

Flat on her stomach on the living-room rug, she was sketching out the outline of the wool flowers. Even the books scattered around her looked bored, just about as bored as Pierrot, who was lying on his side, dozing.

"Study, study, that's all I do," she muttered.

Her mother laughed. "You'd be the biggest dumbbell in Newfoundland if we let you have your way."

"Other kids don't have to study," she said resentfully.

"Anne does."

"Oh, Anne, perfect little Anne," she interrupted. "Nobody else has lessons or homework. We're the only ones."

"That's unfortunate for them. Your father and I are doing our best to be your teachers, so you don't fall too far behind in your studies."

Mary Lou nonchalantly flipped through a schoolbook. "I have to find a gulf in this geography book. A gulf that ends in 'Stream.' "

"I'll help you."

They pored over the map of Newfoundland, a yellow triangle in the light-blue ocean. The big island anchored off the North American continent was a tangle of fjords and promontories. On either side of the Avalon Peninsula, the most populated region, Mary Lou spotted Placentia Bay, where Oderin was, and Trinity Bay. Only a five-kilometre bridge of land kept the peninsula from being cut off from the rest of Newfoundland. But gulfs ending in "Stream?" Not a trace. All she could see was Conception, St. Mary's . . .

"Maybe it's in Canada?" asked her mother.

They turned the page. Suddenly her mother's finger stopped right in the middle of the ocean. "It wouldn't be the Gulf Stream by any chance, would it?" she teased.

"That's it!"

Mrs. McGuire told her about the marine current, but Mary Lou would have none of it.

"How can you have a river of water in the ocean?"

"Just like the wind in the air."

Suddenly, Sarah's singing started up twice as loud in the kitchen. To the connoisseur, a change of rhythm meant Sarah was beginning to knead the dough.

Mrs. McGuire took pity on her daughter. Mary Lou liked bread days most of all.

"You can go in and visit Sarah. I'll call you when it's time for your lessons."

"You're the nicest mummy in the world," Mary Lou burst out.

The heavy kitchen door slammed right behind her, leaving Pierrot just enough time to slip through. He could step lively when his interests were at stake.

"I've come to help you, Sarah!"

"Don't need no help," the old woman grumbled. But her eyes belied her cantankerous look. She swept Mary Lou up in her stiff, well-starched apron that made her look something like an igloo.

The oven was ready. Its stifling heat was mixed with the smell of yeast. Now came time for the real work. Sarah threw the dough on a board. In a great snowstorm of flour, she beat and pushed and tortured the big ball of dough that took on one shape after another – a cloud or a seal, a turtle or a sack of sugar.

Sarah kneaded and transformed and lifted the heavy, malleable lump. As it changed shape, it lost half its volume. Satisfied with her art, she made a face that Mary Lou interpreted as a smile. Next the dough had to be divided up. Sarah dropped a lump of it on the platform scale. Wonder of wonders! This old woman did not know how to read or write, but she could divide the dough in equal parts every time. Each one weighed sixteen ounces, not one more or less.

"Sarah, have you ever been to Saint Pierre and Miquelon?" Mary Lou asked her.

The two neighbouring islands were a haven to French cod-fishermen.

"As I stand before you, I've never set foot off Oderin," the old woman replied proudly.

"Do you know that Papa's coming back today?"

"Everyone in the village knows that."

Mary Lou could hold her tongue no longer. "He's bringing back a secret," she confided in a mysterious voice.

"And what secret is that?"

"I don't know. It's a surprise," she said in an important tone. "He wrote Mummy a letter. I don't think he's bring ing back a thing. I think it's an idea. I bet he's got some good ones."

Jerome, Mary Lou's little brother, burst into the kitchen. Before he got around to begging, Sarah gave him a little ball of dough. He crushed it between his fingers before swallowing it.

"Mummy wants to see you, Mary Lou," he said.

"You're talking with your mouth full."

"You're just saying that because you don't want to study," he declared.

Mary Lou sighed. Ever since the teacher had left Oderin, her parents took time out to teach their daughters English, French, arithmetic and everything else students should know. But Mary Lou preferred her walks on the headland and games with her friends.

"Sarah, what about Tom?"

"What did Tom do now?" she asked. Tom was her grandson.

"Who's teaching him now that Mr. Burke's gone?"

"Nobody at all," Sarah sighed.

"Lucky duck!"

"No, Mary Lou, you're the one who's lucky. Nobody knows how to read in my family."

"But what about Tom's father?"

"He doesn't know how to read, either."

"But he reads the paper every time he comes to see Papa."

"He doesn't know how to read," insisted Sarah. "Tom is the first one who ever had the chance to go to school."

"But I *saw* him," Mary Lou shot back.

"And so you did," Sarah grumbled. And a strange look came over her face.

"See, I'm right," Mary Lou said.

Sarah shot her a fiery glance. Who knew what it meant? But it definitely put a stop to the conversation.

"Just the same, I'd like to be in Tom's shoes," Mary Lou put in.

"If he could learn a thing or two, he'd be a lot better off."

Mary Lou threw her arms around the old woman's neck. "I've got a great idea! I'll teach Tom everything I learn at home, after every lesson."

Sarah smiled one of her rare smiles that lit up her craggy face. "You're a good girl after all."

Mary Lou scampered off to her lessons. Her mother

had never seen her so serious. No use asking too many questions – her zeal might disappear as quickly as it had come. The lesson dragged on, but Mary Lou did not seem tired.

With a glance at the clock, her mother said, "The *Glencoe* will be in soon. You can put away your books."

The ship would be heaving into sight at any moment. As soon as it tacked around the cliffs, Mary Lou would alert her mother. Mary Lou went down to the beach, close to the house, to watch for it.

Soon she began daydreaming, remembering the day Pierrot, her dog, had come to Oderin. She pictured herself on the wharf, a year ago, waiting for her father to return from Saint Pierre and Miquelon, just like today. He had promised a surprise for the entire family. Pierrot turned out to be that surprise.

The gangway had been let down, but no one got off. For a very good reason: an enormous Newfoundland dog was blocking the way.

The dog took one step forward, then retreated two, gazing down at the waves below. People were calling out and pointing at him, and the sailors were pushing and pulling at him with all their might. In a show of determination, he sat down on his haunches and sent up a great howl to heaven.

Mary Lou could not simply stand and watch. She ran towards the boat, and people stepped aside. She went up the gangway and squatted down in front of the dog. They eyed each other in silence, taking time to get acquainted.

The dog made the first move, and it was a friendly one. He yelped a yelp of welcome, put his big furry paw on Mary Lou's arm and wagged his feathery tail. As if signing an oath, he licked her cheek. In return, she threw her arms around his muscular neck and buried her face in his rough fur.

Then she stood and said in a gentle voice, "Come on, boy."

The astonished crowd waited. The dog did not hesitate for an instant. Very dignified, he strode behind her to take possession of his new kingdom: Oderin.

Back home, Mrs. McGuire was not quite sure what to think. She liked dogs, but they already had three, for hunting and watching over the house. An animal that size was a little overwhelming.

Jerome was quite simply terrified. He whimpered fearfully from behind his mother's skirts.

"Do you like my present?" Mr. McGuire asked.

"He's wonderful!" Mary Lou was quick to answer.

"Is he going to get any bigger?" asked Anne, who was not as brave as her sister.

"He'll keep growing," Mr. McGuire informed them. "An adult Newfoundland can weigh up to ninety kilos. But careful, now! He's a French citizen. He doesn't speak the same language we do."

"But he's a Newfoundland," Mary Lou insisted. "He must speak English, because we do."

"He was born on Saint Pierre," her father retorted.

"What's his name?" she asked.

"Pierrot," her father said. "Named after his native island."

With a few long strides, the dog began exploring the big kitchen. He stopped in front of the oven, clearly astonished to see Sarah standing on the table, her arms raised heavenward.

"Find him a bone, Mary Lou," her father told her. "Don't be afraid, Sarah. He's as gentle as a lamb."

Sarah did not believe a word of it, not when she saw the way Pierrot looked at the hambone in Mary Lou's hand. But he sniffed it delicately, then brought his jaws slowly around the bone, and dragged it behind the stove where he could gnaw away to his heart's content.

Later, Mary Lou asked Pierrot, "Do you want to take the tour?"

Holding him by the collar, she guided him through the house. The living-room did not interest him much, and neither did the hallway. Better hurry past the office where her parents were talking. Pierrot should see the sewing room and the tiny chamber they still called the "hospital," from the days when a doctor had lived in the house. Obviously, Pierrot had never climbed a staircase. But he emerged from the experience none the worse for wear and headed straight for the girls' room, seeking out imaginary intruders under the big feather bed. The uproar alerted Mrs. McGuire, who called out from downstairs.

"Mary Lou!"

She jumped. Her mother's voice filtered into her daydream. Someone really *was* calling her.

"Mary Lou!" Mrs. McGuire called again.

Mrs. McGuire was standing on the cliff, silhouetted against the sky. She had changed her clothes and put on her elegant grey skirt. How beautiful she looked! Was it her happiness at her husband's return that put colour in her cheeks and light in her eyes? She was so different from the other women in Oderin. Tom's mother, and Brigitte's, too, were her age, but they had grown old before their time, their bodies bent by hard work.

"Quickly now, the boat's coming!" her mother called from the cliff.

The *Glencoe* would soon be docking. Already they could see the travellers on the bridge. In front stood Phillip McGuire, waving his hand. This time he was alone. Mary Lou felt relieved that he was not bringing back another Newfoundland dog.

CHAPTER SEVEN
The Messenger

MR. MCGUIRE WAS SOON CALLED UPON TO EXplain the surprise he was bringing back from Saint Pierre. Nobody could see it, of course, since it was just an idea.

"On Saint Pierre, Newfoundlands like Pierrot pull handsome little two-wheeled carts. I thought we could get one, too."

The family gathered together in the kitchen, drawn by the smell of baking bread that was almost ready. On a piece of paper, Phillip McGuire sketched out what he had in mind.

"Will you make the cart yourself?" Mary Lou asked.

"We'll ask MacDonald to do it."

That was a common refrain. The old Scots fisherman was a master builder and a skilled carpenter, like all the sailors who built and repaired their own boats. But MacDonald also knew how to repair kettles, cut hair, sweep chimneys and darn socks.

Mary Lou gladly acted as messenger. "Can I go to Mr. MacDonald's place and ask him about the cart?"

"Yes, go ahead," Mr. McGuire agreed.

Escorted by Pierrot, Mary Lou ran almost the whole way. If it were not for the beauty of the landscape, she could have run with her eyes closed – she knew every inch of her island. Everyone on Oderin was her friend – men and women, young and old. This was no great achievement, of course, since there were fewer than three hundred people on the island.

She knew the island was a harsh place. Her parents said that Oderin's land wasn't much good for farming. "Too many rocks growing there already," were her father's words.

Mary Lou skipped along the hard surface of the path. Rock stuck through everywhere. Newfoundland, that gigantic boulder in the North Atlantic, defied the seas and the centuries.

The wind rose up, carrying the scent of spring. Mary Lou felt like singing; there was no reason to be a proper young lady there on the headland. She sat down on a rock and took off her boots. She tied the laces together and threw the boots over her shoulder. Barefoot now, she ran along the round paving stones. The path overlooked the sea, which had broken its chains. The ice was drifting, and the blocks were growing smaller under the sun. Steam rose up, as if suddenly the ocean could breathe freely again. The air was growing thick, opaque, almost white.

Far off to the northeast, above the Grand Banks, the fog was gathering at the spot where the cold Arctic currents met the warm Gulf Stream. Sometimes, when the island caught the tail of a hurricane, Oderin was wrapped in fog for days. The surrounding islands disappeared on the horizon. First to go was Patrice Island, the most distant – the one that belonged to Mr. McGuire. Then Wood Island where, since time immemorial, the inhabitants of Oderin had gone to gather their fuel every autumn.

Mary Lou was glad to see Angus MacDonald's little house rise up before her. Twelve years earlier, the year of her birth, Angus had arrived on Oderin, no one ever knew where from. He'd settled into one of Mr. McGuire's run-down shacks and set about making it as good as new.

Why had he washed up on Oderin's shores? Why had he chosen to settle on an island where he was a complete stranger? All Mary Lou knew was that a rough-and-ready friendship flourished between her father and Angus. Pierrot had limitless veneration for the Scotsman, and as far as Mary Lou was concerned, that was enough.

The old man had the habit of carrying a few sticks of dynamite under his shirt. People said that in winter he kept them warm in his oven. Angus had a passion. He swore he would find copper on the island. Now and again, somewhere on the island, you would hear an explosion. "That's Angus again," the good folk of Oderin would say, shaking their heads at such a dangerous enterprise.

Mr. McGuire was the only one who approved of the project, and sometimes he went along for the ride.

His wife would say in worried tones, "You oughtn't to encourage his folly."

To which he would reply, "They found iron on Belle Island, so why not copper on Oderin?"

In 1893, an English captain had noticed the rusty-coloured rocks that a Newfoundland crew had thrown into the hull for ballast. Those sailors had come from Belle Island, and thanks to them, important deposits of iron were discovered.

"One of these days," Mrs. McGuire said, "Angus is going to blow himself up with his dynamite, and you'll go with him."

"That'll probably be the day he discovers his copper," her husband answered. He was not one to take her fears very seriously.

But today Angus MacDonald was carrying no dynamite under his shirt, which reassured Mary Lou. She explained the reason for her visit and gave him her father's sketch of what was to become Pierrot's dog-cart.

"Tell your father I'll help him. I'll be there tomorrow."

"Thanks!" she called out, already on her way.

Carried along by her light heart, Mary Lou ran up the slope of the headland, hanging on to every foothold. What a reward at the top! Far below, the waves attacked the granite cliffs, then fell back in white cascades, their energy spent. In the hollows of the rocks, green stems stuck their heads above the greyish moss. A few more weeks and they would make fine flowery bouquets. Turning her back to the sea, Mary Lou moved slowly through a swampy area. Her bare feet sank into the ground like a cold, wet sponge. Too bad! At least her feet would dry more quickly than her shoes.

A strange plant grew in this desert of scruffy grass. It was called the pitcher plant, and it was as hardy as a pine and proud in its abundant growth. Each plant bore a single flower that scarcely opened, and whose purple petals pointed at the ground. The Indians called it frog-grass because, like a frog, it fed on insects.

Mary Lou bent down and freed the leaves of the pitcher plant from the moss. They were as thick as her finger. She scraped the inside of one of them with her nail. Stiff hairs pointing downward imprisoned the careless insects that sought shelter there and tried to drink the rainwater in the tiny basin.

After they drowned, the victims were devoured by this horrible carnivore. Mary Lou was not sure she could forgive such cruelty. And to think that Queen Victoria, forty years before, had chosen the purple pitcher plant to decorate the Newfoundland penny. Even queens made mistakes! But these were the first flowers of the season, so Mary Lou picked herself a big bouquet.

Back at the house, she was full of questions. "Where do Newfoundland dogs come from?" she asked.

"Most people think that they descended from Pyrenees dogs," her father explained. "Perhaps the Basques brought them here at the time of the French colonies. The sailors liked them because they made excellent lifeguards. Their thick, woolly fur did not get water-logged right away, and it kept them warm if they fell into the sea. Since they're strong and loyal, they were used to carry mail, just like Huskies or Eskimo dogs."

"Are they always black?" Mrs. McGuire asked. "I thought I saw some with white spots."

"You get a few white ones, but most are black, like Labs, their smaller cousins."

As he talked, Mr. McGuire pushed his glasses up on his forehead and read the mail that Tom had brought a little while earlier.

"Look, here's a letter from Uncle Paul."

He frowned. Mrs. McGuire shot him a troubled glance, and Mary Lou sensed a mystery. Uncle Paul never used to write so often, and this was the third time the *Glencoe* had brought disturbing news from St. John's.

A shadow crossed Mr. McGuire's face, but not for long. He showed them an envelope, and on it Mary Lou could read David's handwriting.

"This letter and I both travelled on the *Glencoe*, and I didn't even know it," said Mr. McGuire.

Mary Lou hid the letter until much later, when she could read it at her leisure, sheltered under the quilt, the pages scattered all about her.

Reading out loud, throwing in her own questions and comments, Mary Lou told her pet seal of her older brother's adventures. The seal kept his special status only because her father would not let Pierrot sleep in their room. He had a place of his own in the shed. According to her father, his fur would keep him warm. The seal, more passive than Pierrot, was willing to listen to Mary Lou's secrets.

It seemed that David was having one adventure after another. He had visited a canning plant and had even set foot on a warship, because the father of one of his friends was an officer aboard. Ned, Uncle Paul's son and their favourite cousin, wrote to him from time to time. Ned was twenty-one. He was studying at the University of Dublin in Ireland. At the very end, as a P.S., David wrote these words: *Father Cox came to see me last week at school.*

And that was all. Father Cox was an important figure in their lives. As Burin's priest, he spent months travelling across his enormous parish. Every time he came to Oderin, he stayed at the McGuires' place.

Mary Lou tried to imagine the conversation between her wilful, fiery brother and the saintly priest. Father Cox deserved more than a quick line or two at the bottom of the page.

CHAPTER EIGHT

All Aboard!

MRS. MCGUIRE WAS WORKING IN THE GARDEN with her daughters. Her garden was the prettiest and best kept in all of Oderin. You had to hoe and weed and plant and water, she said. But most of all, you had to love your garden if you wanted the plants to come up and the flowers to open at their appointed time.

"Just like with children," she summed up.

For once, Anne was not afraid to get her hands dirty. But even with mud on the tip of her nose and her hair tied up in a scarf, she looked quite lady-like. Mary Lou was less elegant, but just as enthusiastic, burying her hands in the earth. And with his little shovel, Jerome readied a tiny flowerbed. Already he imagined the sunflowers raising their yellow heads.

Mrs. McGuire hummed their favourite tune, and soon the girls' voices took up the refrain. Suddenly weary, she wiped her forehead with her hand and sighed, "I wonder who will pick my roses this year?"

She had been thinking out loud. Taken aback, her daughters asked, "What do you mean, who *will* pick your roses?"

"Did I say that? Are you sure?" Her face suddenly looked careworn. Then she grabbed a startled Jerome and said, "Come, darling. We have to pick up all these little stones."

But she did not sound happy.

Patiently, she helped Jerome, spoke to him gently and

brought a smile back to his worried eyes. Anne did not give the incident much thought, but Mary Lou was too preoccupied to give the weeds more than half-hearted attention.

"You lazybones," Anne said. "You have to work faster than that!"

"I'll work just as fast as I want to!" Mary Lou shot back, standing up suddenly. "Since you don't like the way I work, you can finish without me!"

Anne was outraged. She tried to stop her sister, but her mother stepped in.

"Let her go," Mrs. McGuire said.

Mary Lou sought shelter in her father's office. Absent-mindedly, Mr. McGuire motioned her to come in, even though Thomas Griffith, Tom's father, was sitting solidly in the leather chair, holding the newspaper with an iron grip, looking highly absorbed.

Jerome had left his paper and crayons on a low table. At loose ends, Mary Lou sat down on the carpet and made a few sketches of her dog. Pierrot sleeping, Pierrot gnawing a bone, Pierrot with the three spaniels barking at him. Like her father, she had a gift for drawing.

She had almost finished her sketch when her father's deep voice broke the silence.

"I've finished now, Thomas."

Mr. Griffith did not move a muscle. Perhaps he knew how to read after all and was finishing the article. He folded the paper methodically and got up as Mary Lou's father marked an X at the bottom of the sheet.

"Sign here and everything will be taken care of."

Mr. Griffith took the pen in his big hand and bent over. Slowly, with much application, he wrote *Thomas Griffith*, with plenty of flourishes. He thanked her father profusely and lingered to discuss the events of the day in detail. Then he moved on to the weather, a subject of conversation that never ran dry, just as important for a fisherman as for a farmer.

As soon as Mr. Griffith left, Mary Lou burst out, "Sarah said Mr. Griffith doesn't know how to read."

"Didn't you see him read?" her father answered with a smile.

"But Sarah was very sure. She said Tom was the first one in the family to go to school."

Mr. McGuire had no choice but to reveal the mystery. Mary Lou was just too stubborn, and she might embarrass Mr. Griffith.

"I'll tell you the truth. Thomas doesn't know how to read. But he's a proud man and he doesn't want anyone to suspect as much. He has his son tell him what's in the paper. He thinks I haven't noticed."

"I won't say a thing," she promised, proud to be sharing a grown-up's secret with her father. "You know," she added, "I promised Sarah I'd teach Tom everything that you and mother teach me."

"What does Tom think about it?" he asked.

"He doesn't know yet. I'm going to go see him soon."

Poor boy, how could he resist Mary Lou? her father thought with a smile.

Just then Jerome burst into the room. "The cart is here!"

In no time, the McGuire family had assembled on the porch. Angus MacDonald, dressed in a bulky sweater and sailor's boots, was moving towards them, towing the strangest contraption anyone had ever seen. It was a sort of boat on wheels complete with rough bench and side-litters that made it look something like a schooner, especially since Angus had used what was left of a can of iron-grey enamel paint on it, so that it was the colour of a ship's hull.

"It's great!" the younger members of the family all agreed.

Mr. McGuire bit the stem of his pipe. His wife looked worried. Was the cart stable enough?

They looked for Pierrot to hitch him up to the cart, but he had vanished. Perhaps he knew what was in store for him. Everyone filed into the kitchen for the traditional cup of tea. In a show of authority, Sarah produced a pair of scissors and deposited Jerome on a stool.

"While you're at it, give him a good trim."

The time had come for Jerome's first man's haircut. In those days, boys wore their hair long until they were five. Angus, the island barber, did not have to be asked twice. He slipped his hand under his shirt, produced a stick of dynamite, and placed it on the table.

"Since I was down this way," he said in a matter-of-fact voice, "I thought I'd try my luck at Broken Mast Creek. There's got to be copper there somewhere."

"Must be," Mr. McGuire agreed. "I'll go with you."

At the sight of the explosive, Sarah let out a cry. She stepped back – right onto the tail of the cat, who scampered off with a yelp of outrage.

Anne and Mary Lou went off to find Pierrot and led him back triumphantly. Anne looked at Jerome's shorn head and exclaimed, "You're much better that way!"

"You look just like David!" Mary Lou added. For her, that was the highest compliment.

"But his ears stick out!" his mother lamented.

She was right. Jerome put on a sorry look, but his father said that prominent ears were a sign of intelligence.

"My neck's cold," concluded the object of all this attention.

Everyone went outside to hitch up Pierrot. He was delighted to be of service. Back on Saint Pierre, he had often transported children, and he behaved like a perfect gentleman. Everyone wanted to take a ride, including Mrs. McGuire.

Pierrot, with a proud expression and beating tail, stretched his muscles to the limit and galloped off. What a show of energy! The passengers had to hang on to the cart for dear life. They were knocked around like stones in the surf, and nothing could have been more fun. After an hour, Mr. McGuire decided that Pierrot had had enough. The dog seemed just as fresh as at the beginning of the exercise, but no one was about to challenge his orders.

The party broke up. Despite Mrs. McGuire's protests, her husband went with Angus to Broken Mast Creek. Phillip McGuire even had the privilege of carrying the dynamite.

The very next day, Pierrot was trotting along the road with Mary Lou in the cart, singing at the top of her lungs. Together, they went visiting. They showed off just a little; in Oderin, no one had such a magnificent coach-and-four. Everyone else had to settle for a regular boat.

They reached her friend Brigitte's house. Brigitte was out in front with her mother, hanging up the laundry. Her father, with two of his sons, was working by the sheep pen. Today was an important day. All the animals had to be shorn, and their wool would be made into blankets and clothes. Usually Mary Lou loved to watch the show, almost as much as she loved to watch Mrs. Jarvis card the wool with a big, metal-toothed comb, or Brigitte, skilled beyond her years, spin it on the wheel and turn the rough wool into silky skeins.

But today Mary Lou had no use for sheep. She had come to introduce Pierrot and his cart to the Jarvis family.

"Can I try?" Brigitte asked.

"If Pierrot says it's okay," Mary Lou answered.

Pierrot asked for nothing better. He trotted off gently, circled the house and returned with a great show of pomp, head high, stepping along with much dignity.

Suddenly he spotted a tomcat on the front steps, its tail in the air and its fur standing up. The enemy had to be disposed of!

Two giant leaps were enough to empty the cart of its passenger. Flat on her stomach on the stones, Brigitte burst into tears. Mary Lou threw herself around the dog's neck, which took a certain amount of courage, since Pierrot was totally out of control.

But another cat appeared and Pierrot took a quick turn. Mary Lou got off no easier than Brigitte.

The sheep began to stampede. Mr. Jarvis was furious, and his wife went to put the cats in the house as quickly as she could.

The cart ended on its side in the ditch next to the road. Pierrot was lying down with his tongue hanging out. It was no easy task to free him and get him to his feet. Mary Lou dusted off her dress a little and apologized to Mr. Jarvis. Then, with as much poise as she could muster, she took her place in the cart again.

Pierrot lowered his head.

"He knows I'm in charge," she declared.

"I think it's because of the cats," said one of Brigitte's little brothers.

On her way to Tom's house, Mary Lou met up with Ben. She did not care much for the young fisherman, and her feelings were seconded by Pierrot, who growled threateningly and swerved to the side.

By a stroke of luck, the cart remained right side up, and Mary Lou kept her place inside. But why did Ben look at her with such angry eyes? She did not have the time to talk to him. Tom was working outside repairing a net, and he called out to her.

"Hey, hello there, Mary Lou!"

Naturally, he was very enthusiastic about the cart. He took a short ride and drove Pierrot with great authority, commenting on Angus's work in technical terms that were just as incomprehensible as they were impressive.

"Did you meet Ben?" he asked. "My father might take me fishing this year for real. He didn't say no, and neither did my uncle. Ben came specially to tell me about it, because he knows how much I want to go."

Tom had had enough of repairing nets and drying fish with the women. He wanted to be a real member of the crew.

"But what about school?" Mary Lou protested.

"School? There isn't any more school. That's the point."

She gathered her courage. "I've decided to teach you everything I learn at home."

Tom was speechless. The only sound was the surf booming. Finally, he got over his surprise. Trying not to hurt her feelings, he said, “Thanks anyway, but I’m really not one for studies.”

“Your grandmother wants you to do it—and that makes two of us. We’ll start with reading. You’ll see, it’ll be fun.”

To be taught reading, and by a girl on top of it! The McGuires prestige helped a little, and Tom did admire her father. But all the same, there were limits!

Mary Lou had never even imagined she might be turned down. She began rummaging through the cart for her book, slate and chalk, the tools of her new trade.

After all, Tom said to himself, why not? Though he wanted to fish with his father, he had another, more distant, grander dream. He had never told a soul about it: he wanted to be a sea-going captain. To reach his goal, it would not hurt to know as much as possible about everything.

“All right,” he finally agreed.

Tom was intelligent, but he cared for little else but the sea. He had trouble getting interested in the refinements of language. After all, what did nuances matter as long as people understood you?

They sat down on a bench, and the lesson began. With great pains, Tom managed to follow Mary Lou, but after half an hour, he felt he had worked more than a whole day in a fishing boat.

They sat down on a bench, and the lesson began.

CHAPTER NINE

Pierrot, Where Have You Gone?

ONE DAY, AS SPRING MELTED THE ICE IN THE bay, disaster struck. Pierrot disappeared.

Mary Lou called him in vain. The little cart sat forlornly in front of the shed.

Mary Lou resigned herself to walking to Tom's house for his lessons, but her heart was not in teaching. So Tom offered to help search, and together they crisscrossed the island. They looked into sheds where Pierrot might have been inadvertently locked up and asked questions of whoever happened along.

"Pierrot's dead!" she said in a tiny, mournful voice. "I know it, he's dead. Or else he's hurt and he can't get back!"

"We'll find him," said Mr. McGuire. He had talked over the disappearance with the neighbours, but was still no closer to discovering the dog's whereabouts.

Mr. McGuire organized a search party. Soon all the islanders were alerted, and they looked for the dog everywhere they went. The three spaniels of the McGuire household were part of the search, moved by the cautious friendship they felt for their dog brother.

The spaniels followed a trail down to the wharf. With their sad eyes, they seemed to say, "Here it is. This is as far as Pierrot went. Believe us. We know what we're talking about."

"He went swimming and he drowned!" Mary Lou concluded in a state of desperation.

"A Newfoundland can't drown," her mother told her.

"He'll come back," Anne assured her. "You just don't disappear like that. Pierrot has to be *somewhere.*"

All that common sense did not convince Mary Lou, and her tears began to fall again. "I knew something bad was going to happen. I loved Pierrot too much. We were so happy!"

"You still love him and he'll come back," Anne promised. "Pierrot's got to be somewhere."

"But where?" sobbed Mary Lou, nestled in her older sister's arms.

She finally fell asleep. That night the seal, abandoned, lay forlornly in the corner.

Three days passed. Slowly, everyone got used to the idea of Pierrot's disappearance.

Everyone but Mary Lou. She stopped talking, picked at her food, and it took all her effort to keep from crying. Inconsolable, she wandered on the headlands, refusing Anne's and Jerome's companionship. Weary and discouraged, Mary Lou was returning from a walk along the cliffs when she glimpsed someone hiding behind a copse of trees. It was Tom. He looked upset as he stepped out from his shelter. His voice was dry and mournful.

"Listen, Mary Lou, I know where your dog is. He's on a boat sailing to Europe."

"Are you sure?"

"Yes."

Pierrot wasn't dead! That was the most important thing.

Tom explained, "A fisherman took him to Placentia and sold him to a Portuguese sailor who was going abroad."

"Why, Tom, why?"

"You can get a lot of money for a Newfoundland, and people on Oderin aren't very rich."

"But who did it?"

She had always considered the islanders her friends: Tom, Alice, David, Brigitte and the others – even Angus, the outsider. She thought they liked her, too.

"Who did it?" she asked again.

"I think it would be better if you didn't know."

Suddenly she felt her world slipping away from her. Things would never be the same again.

Later that day, Mary Lou climbed onto her father's lap as she had done as a child. But her pain was more than childish disappointment. "Don't you see, Papa, someone on the island did it, someone we know. But Tom won't tell me who."

"Tom is right," her father replied. "It's better if you don't know, and if you don't try to find out, either."

"It's terrible. I'll suspect everyone."

"We might be able to catch up to Pierrot. I'll try and find out the name of the boat. I'll write to the fitters who own it. We'll try. There's still hope."

Suddenly, she burst out, "Papa, could it be Angus?"

Mr. McGuire stiffened. "Angus? Why Angus?"

"Because he's not from Oderin. He's an outsider. He's different from us."

"Mary Lou, how could you say that? Angus is an honest man."

He frowned and looked angry. "You must never let those kinds of thoughts into your heart. I'll go and see Tom. He was very wise for a boy his age. He might be willing to tell me more. I'll do what I can."

CHAPTER TEN

Bon Voyage!

SARAH WALKED ALONG SLOWLY – MUCH TOO slowly for Mary Lou's liking. Mary Lou ran ahead impatiently, then returned; she must have made the trip three times. They were off to see Mr. Griffith, Sarah's son. Mary Lou flew this way and that, talking non-stop, not bothering to wait for an answer.

"Sarah, will Tom be home, do you think? I can't wait to tell him the news! Have you ever been to St. John's?"

"No, never," Sarah said, the picture of patience. "I've told you before, I've never stepped off Oderin."

Mary Lou stopped in her tracks. "But I can't believe it. Not even to Burin or Placentia?"

"Oderin is a better place," Sarah said firmly.

"How do you know? You've never been anywhere else."

"Your father says so, and my son does, too."

"I'm going to go around the world," Mary Lou declared.

"Oh? Tomorrow or the next day?"

Mary Lou could not tell her when. She laughed. "As soon as possible. I'm starting with St. John's, tomorrow."

The two Thomases, father and son, were building a dory that was almost complete. While Sarah went inside to drink a cup of tea, Mary Lou admired her friend's masterpiece. Attaching the oarlocks was all that remained to be done. Tom had made them out of spruce roots that would bend but not break.

"It's great," Mary Lou said sincerely.

"It's nothing really," Tom protested. "Every fellow in Newfoundland knows how to build one."

"David doesn't," she said. Her admiration for her brother had not blinded her completely.

Tom shrugged his shoulders. "David is different."

She frowned. "No, he's like you, like everybody else."

"No," Tom contradicted her. "He's changed and you'll change, too. You'll go and study in town. You'll be a proper young lady. I'll just stay plain old Tom."

"But David's your friend."

"Not anymore."

Tom was right, Mary Lou had to admit. A world of difference separated the boyhood friends. Tom's face looked bitter and hard. How could he escape the fate that awaited every young man on Oderin? He had to start earning his living early.

To lighten the atmosphere, Mary Lou asked, "Do you remember when David and you went on your expedition?"

Did he ever! Three years earlier, Tom and David's journey had set the island on its ear. They had set out to circumnavigate Newfoundland in an old rowboat that they had recaulked. David had been reading a biography of Magellan, and his stories had set Tom's imagination on fire. They sailed off to explore the ten thousand kilometres of coastline, stopping in the ports at the end of the bays, living off what they took from the sea. On the dawn of the third day, the journey of thirteen hundred stopovers ended abruptly off Argentia, between Trepassey Bay and Cappahaden, the most dangerous spot on the island. Through the ages, countless ships had met their fate there, breaking up on the reefs. Exhausted and soaked to the skin, the two boys took turns bailing after their boat, too, ran aground. Still, they toughed it out, and were none too happy to be fished out like cod in a net.

But Tom and David lived in different worlds now. And the worst thing, Mary Lou said to herself, is that David has changed more than Tom.

Tom did not like thinking of that ruined friendship or that unfortunate expedition. Spitefully, he told her, "Your father will send you to boarding school for sure next year."

"You really think so?"

"You'll have to go since we don't have any more teachers here."

She asked thoughtfully, "Brigitte's my best friend. Do you think what happened to David and you will happen to Brigitte and me?"

"Just like between David and me," he said cruelly.

"I don't want it to happen! I don't want it to happen!"

Her words were a cry from the bottom of her heart, and Tom was sorry he'd been so harsh. "Think of it, Mary Lou," he said. "Can you imagine me in a city school?"

No, she could not picture Tom in the streets of St. John's or Halifax, where the sea was tamed. To live in a city, he would have to shorten his stride and limit his horizons.

"My father is going to St. John's tomorrow," she said, "and I get to go with him."

They hesitated, and came to a halt in mid-sentence. Anne and David had already visited the capital. Now it was Mary Lou's turn. She felt a little embarrassed announcing the news to Tom, who did not share the same privilege.

"Don't worry about me," he assured her. "One day I'll go a lot farther than St. John's. I'll go wherever the salt water flows, like the old schooner captains used to say. Just like them, I'll sell my fish to Brazil, Portugal, everywhere. I'll travel a lot farther than you, my girl, and I won't be taking the train! I'll have my own boat, you'll see."

Then Sarah called out to them. It was time to go.

Tom added proudly, "I wish I could take you in my dory right now. When you come back, it'll be finished."

"It looks great already," she answered, running to catch up to Sarah, who was beginning to grumble.

The train was slowing to a stop. Mary Lou pressed her nose against the glass. She wished she had a thousand eyes to take in all the sights. This was St. John's!

City streets whipped past. She saw countless houses, more than she ever thought could be crowded into one small space. Then came a row of stores with dark windows, so narrow that four or five of them could fit into their big house on Oderin. Each one was like a tiny cave.

The brakes squealed. The passengers leaned to the left, then to the right, then forward and backward at each jerk. The locomotive gave a kind of high whinny, like a sea monster. Then it blew, spit and came to a halt in front of a red wooden building that was new and shiny. After all, the railway was only four years old.

"Hurry up, Mary Lou," Anne said, very excited.

Mary Lou was too dumbstruck to move. All this bustle, dust and noise got the better of her. The trip on the *Glencoe* was enchanting. But when it came to the journey on the narrow track, with the train cars banging this way and that, she quickly changed her mind about travelling.

"Come on, you silly country girl," said Anne, who had

already spent a month in St. John's the summer before with Uncle Paul.

Mrs. McGuire gathered up the bags and trunks. Her hair was falling in her face, and her hat was on crooked, but her eyes were shining with adventure. On the station platform, Mary Lou spotted Uncle Paul and Aunt Lucie with their two daughters, Maureen and Nancy. She knew them well, since they came to Oderin every summer. But who was that young man with them?

Soon she found herself on the platform, face to face with this tall stranger. He bowed from on high, extended a long, bony hand and said, "Mary Lou, I presume? My name is Ned."

For the last few years, her cousin Ned, Maureen and Nancy's older brother, had been studying in Dublin, where young Newfoundlanders of Irish descent were sometimes sent. That was why Mary Lou had never met him before. She bent her knee in a half-curtsey to show that a country girl could have as good manners as city folk.

A great clatter of wagons carrying the travellers' trunks was heard in the courtyard.

"Horses!" cried Mary Lou.

She had never seen a horse except in picture books. Then came another new sight: a sort of carriage without benches.

"Oh, Paul!" her mother cried. "You bought a car!"

Ned put on goggles, a driver's cap and sat down behind the wheel. Aunt Lucie, Mother and the four girls squeezed in as best they could on the high seats, one on top of the other. Uncle Paul took off his jacket, rolled up his sleeves, leaned over the front of the car and grabbed the crank. He turned it as hard as he could until the sweat shone on his red forehead. Finally, the motor coughed! It growled, stopped, then sprang to life again, and this time its purring was steady. Paul quickly hoisted himself up next to his son, and they chugged off down the street. The skittish horses would just have to watch their step! Mary Lou loved the horses, but she was not so sure about automobiles. Did you have to wind them up like mechanical toys or hold the rudder like a boat? Amazing as it sounded, she, the dare-devil of Oderin, was afraid. But she did not admit it, especially since everyone else, even Anne and her mother, seemed to be in seventh heaven.

Her cousins' house felt small and narrow. Its stuffy smell contrasted with the fresh air and sunshine of her Oderin home.

She pointed at a strange black box attached to the wall. "What's that?" she asked.

Maureen and Nancy burst out laughing as Ned explained, "That's a telephone."

Mary Lou bit her lip, angry at her teasing cousin and those giggling girls.

By the time supper was served, she was too exhausted by the trip and the new sights to be hungry. After dessert, the four girls went out into the yard. Three of them, already perfect young ladies, made for their favourite spots: the old oak, the wooden bench and the summer house where they had once played dolls.

Mary Lou drifted off on her own. She saw the sea at the end of every street, but it was a tamed sea. The houses thrown together with their yards and gardens, the stone walls and fences that closed off the horizon – how different it was. On her island, she could climb trees and run across the headland, but here she hardly dared to move.

She didn't want to dirty her pretty new dress, and her expensive shoes hurt her heels.

If Brigitte could see me, she thought to herself, *she'd feel sorry for me*!

Suddenly someone was standing beside her. She looked up and met Ned's understanding eyes.

"You don't like St. John's, do you?"

She shook her head.

"Come on," he said, "I'm sure we can find a part of town that you'll like."

She followed him docilely out of the garden, then through the narrow streets leading down towards the harbour. Among the houses, she could see schooners, trawlers and ships of all tonnages.

Ned liked this half-wild girl. During supper, she had not opened her mouth except to ask a few extraordinary questions and make judgements about people and things that were both unexpected and wise. She was naive, yet demanding. Compared to life in St. John's, she offered the originality and straightforwardness that Ned had always admired in Mary Lou's father.

They left the St. John's business district behind. The street bordered a wooden jetty where boats were tied up. The wind was rising and the sun lowering on the horizon beyond the city. Dark and squat, Cabot's Tower was sketched against the sky.

"Cabot was from Genoa, in Italy," Ned explained. "He claimed Newfoundland in 1497, in the name of England. After fifty-four days of sailing, he discovered nothing but cod banks. He called his ship the *Matthew*, and it had a crew of eighteen, no bigger than one of these boats."

Mary Lou marvelled at Cabot's bravery. Ned went on,

"When he first laid eyes on the coastline, Cabot cried, 'Buona vista' – 'beautiful view' in Italian, his language."

"I can see why," said Mary Lou.

"It's a fine spot, isn't it? And for his troubles, King Henry VII gave him ten pounds sterling, about forty dollars."

"Was he the first explorer in Newfoundland?"

"Oh, no! Sailors had discovered the Grand Banks long before that, and they used to drop anchor here. The Middle Ages were a hungry time, and fish helped feed people. The fishermen came from Europe: Basques, Bretons, Portuguese and Englishmen."

"Then Cabot really didn't discover anything at all," Mary Lou interrupted.

"But he did. Until then, the fishermen kept the secret to themselves. Cabot was actually looking for the passage to India and the land of spices."

"I suppose the king was disappointed."

"Not really. Over the next century, Queen Elizabeth did everything she could to encourage the fisheries. She even made a law that forced Englishmen to eat fish twice a week. She needed sailors for her warships, and building up the fishing fleet was a way of training men without spending a cent. Besides, her enemies, the Spaniards, were willing to buy cod from her. That was a way of getting their gold from Mexico and Peru into her country."

As they talked, they reached the foot of a forbidding-looking tower. A copper plaque attached to the wall celebrated the glory of Marconi.

"Who's this Marconi?" Mary Lou asked. "An explorer like Cabot?"

"Marconi invented the wireless telegraph. In this very tower, he received the first message that his helpers sent him from Poldhu, in England, in December, 1901."

"Once Papa showed me a photo of a man in a long coat and a silk hat flying a kite. He said he was a friend of Marconi's."

"That's because they used kites to receive the messages."

Ned led her towards the sea. There, as on Oderin, they discovered endless vistas. The waves swelled up and spent their energy, then were born again, as far as the eye could see.

"Right here," said Ned, raising his voice over the wind, "we're halfway between London and New York. Those rocks over there are called Cape Spear. They're the closest the New World comes to the Old."

"Look!" Mary Lou cried. "The fishermen are coming back!"

Three dories were rowing their way between the black cliffs. Their yellow and white hulls bobbed on the choppy dark-green waves. One after the other, the dories dipped their pointed hulls into the sea. Ever watchful, the men needed all their experience to fight the currents that swirled beneath the water's surface.

"It must have been hard back in those days to come in on a sailing ship," said Mary Lou.

"But they still do it," Ned answered. "Every spring, the entire Portuguese fishing fleet docks here."

He described the yearly visit of what people called the "white fleet." In March or April, the ships lined up along the docks, as the foreign sailors swarmed through the town. There could be as many as two thousand of them at a time, and their colourful language with its many vowel sounds brightened up the town. They were excellent sailors who kept a four-century-long tradition alive by dropping anchor in the protected harbour of St. John's, after coming to fish for cod on the Grand Banks.

Ned explained, "They left us plenty of names in their own language – village names like Portugal Cove. And Fermuse, which means beautiful; Fogo, fire; Aquaforte, Baie de Verde and Baccalieu."

"The French go to Saint Pierre and Miquelon," Mary Lou replied, proud of her knowledge. "That's where Pierrot is from."

"Have you heard anything about Pierrot?" Ned asked. He already knew about the dog's disappearance.

She described how lost and betrayed she felt. Someone from Oderin had sold her dog for money, while all the time she had considered everyone on the island to be her friend. For a long time, Ned kept silent, then finally he spoke.

"You're the daughter of Phillip McGuire, Mary Lou. You have everything and they have almost nothing."

Pretty soon he'll be telling me that the thief was right to steal Pierrot, she thought to herself.

"You have to understand them," Ned went on, "and forgive."

Over the past few years, Ned had grown aware of the injustice that kept the fishermen's sons in ignorance and poverty while he, David, Anne and Mary Lou led an easier life. Phillip and Paul McGuire were concerned with these problems, but a lot more had to be done.

"One day," Ned promised in a fiery voice, "every son of Newfoundland will have his chance."

"And every daughter, too!" Mary Lou added, thinking of her friend Brigitte.

Turning their backs to the sea, they headed towards town. Mary Lou gasped with admiration. During their walk, night had fallen, and now lights twinkled in every window.

"What a big city!" she said in a low voice.

"Silly girl! There are a lot bigger cities than St. John's."

CHAPTER ELEVEN
Home at Last

THE *GLENCOE* SLIPPED GENTLY TOWARDS THE dock. Mary Lou's journey was about to end. A photograph that Uncle Paul had taken showed her in well-polished shoes and an embroidered dress. She decided it was not such a bad picture after all. It would remind her of the trip and her first stay in St. John's.

For the first time in her life, she was returning home with a harvest of new experiences. St. John's was magnificent with all its wonders and its harbour, but Oderin was her home, her world. On the wharf, she saw her family: David standing slender and tall, waving his hand. Jerome at his side, jumping up and down like a mountain goat. Pierrot was the only one missing.

Mary Lou leaned on the rail and gazed upon the houses scattered across the island in the rough beauty of the landscape. The fishermen had returned an hour earlier. At the end of their ropes, their dories danced in the water.

On the shore, men, women and children salted fish and

hung them on scaffolding, where they would dry in the sun. The sight, so peaceful yet so grand, had never seemed so beautiful. It was as if she were seeing it for the very first time.

There was a special traveller on board the ship: Father Cox, the priest of Burin, who had come to visit his farflung parish. He came to Oderin two or three times a year, and when he did, it was time to man the battle-stations at the McGuire house. Two days were spent getting the old dwelling into shape. The big window that faced the west was opened, and sunlight and fresh air banished the musty odour of the guest room.

But this time, no preparations had been made for his arrival, because Mrs. McGuire and her daughters were on board the *Glencoe*, too. Who would take out the salty, herb-smelling sheets? Who would give the word to start rolling the pie crusts and kill the chickens? Who would arrange for more loaves to be baked? Who would dig deep into the basement storehouse and come up with the preserves and jams and garden vegetables still wrapped in black earth?

The *Glencoe* struck the wharf with a thud, and David grabbed the trunks. This time, all Father Cox's needs would be attended to, thanks to Sarah. In Mrs. McGuire's absence, Sarah had taken the initiative and prepared the house to receive family and guests. The McGuire dwelling shone. It was a comfortable place, a happy house, and Father Cox was welcomed with the usual ceremony.

Father Cox was a saintly man, respected by the sailors, for he shared their rough life. When he had graduated from the Seminary, he'd had plenty of illusions. Visiting the sick had always conjured up exemplary images. He imagined a priest in cassock and surplice sailing across a silky smooth sea, speeded on by strong-armed oarsmen. Reality turned out to be somewhat different. People did not consider the weather when they neared death, and often he found himself wearing a sailor's slicker and boots. He had been shipwrecked twice. His boat had gone down, and he had had to walk on the ice floes. There was no better man than he for working the pump when a dory was taking on water. But he would not trade a minute of it, for such was a priest's work in Newfoundland in 1912.

In Oderin, he went about meeting his parishioners. There were confessions in the evening, Mass the next day, no baptism this time but a marriage between a cod-trawler's daughter and a young fisherman from Nova Scotia. Then Father Cox sailed off again, promising to return in the autumn.

Mary Lou was eager to tell Brigitte about her trip to St. John's. She ran along the narrow path. The noisy, happy house rose up before her. The capelins, used for fertilizer, were rotting in the fields in the summer heat, and Mary Lou wrinkled her nose. On the sunny side of the house, sheltered from the wind, the Griffiths had heaped up the earth they had patiently gathered and carried there in baskets. Carrots, cabbages and beets fought for a place in the sun in the garden. Whisky, the dog, scarcely lifted his head as Mary Lou went past. The log tied to his neck kept him from chasing the sheep. It did not look as though he had the energy for it anyway.

Mary Lou made straight for the open door, through which children, flies and cats swarmed in.

"Hey, Brigitte!"

"Hello, Mary Lou!"

They had so many things to talk about! Brigitte could scarcely believe the things her friend described. But Mary Lou showed her the black-and-white photographs, and proved without a doubt that she had not dreamed up her extraordinary adventure. In front of the cathedral, there she was in an embroidered dress and new boots.

"I had on a red belt," she added.

Mrs. Jarvis asked, "Did Father Cox leave already, Mary Lou?"

"Yes, ma'am."

Mrs. Jarvis gave a sigh, and Brigitte explained, "Mama was hoping to have her baby before he left because of the baptism. Now she'll have to wait another two months, at least."

That very night little Martha was born, another joy for the Griffith family.

CHAPTER TWELVE
Pierrot Sends Word

"HERE'S A LETTER FROM PIERROT!"

David came rushing in from the living-room, waving a letter, as Mary Lou ran down the stairs four steps at a time.

"Pierrot wrote us a letter?" she asked.

"Not exactly. The letter is from the ship-owner Papa wrote to."

Together they examined the fancy paper with the name of a large English shipping company on the letterhead. A certain Mr. Raleigh declared in polite tones that he had undertaken an investigation and located the dog. He was sending him home via Brazil and Martinique.

"Pierrot's sailing the seas right now," David said. "He might be in Rio, or even in the Antilles."

Mary Lou's blank look told him the names meant nothing to her.

"Don't you know where Rio is?" he asked.

"No."

"What about Liverpool?"

"No."

"Well, Pierrot knows more than you do."

He spun the globe in their father's office and stopped it when he reached Liverpool. Then came Rio di Janeiro and Fort-de-France, the capital of Martinique. Exhaustive commentary accompanied every location.

Very impressed, Mary Lou declared, "In Fort-de-France, Pierrot will feel at home since they speak French there. But do you think he'll be seasick?"

"Newfoundlanders can weather any storm – and that goes for their dogs, too."

"What about Oderin?" she asked. "Show me Oderin."

They quickly found the Avalon Peninsula between its twin bays, but it was so small they could scarcely make it out. Oderin, Mary Lou's whole world, did not even appear on the map.

"It's too small," David declared.

Mary Lou pointed to a spot in the North Atlantic. "There's the Gulf Stream, and this is the Labrador Current."

David laughed and ran his knowledgeable fingers over the blue expanse of the ocean. "I think the Vikings must have crossed here, with Eric the Red and his son Leif."

Norway, Iceland, Greenland and perhaps Labrador

and Newfoundland had all been stopovers on the Vikings' voyages. As if he were standing on the prow of a drakkar, David rhapsodized about the long Scandinavian boats shaped like sea-monsters, with their shields sparkling in the sun on both sides of the vessels.

Ned came in at the end of the conversation and interrupted them. "We got word from St. John's. We'll be leaving tomorrow."

"We?" David repeated, intrigued.

"Your parents and I."

Ned had his grown-up look on, and that worried Mary Lou. Uncle Paul's letters usually meant nothing but trouble for the family.

But by the next morning, the mood had changed. Mrs. McGuire suggested, "Let's take the children with us to Placentia."

A shadow crossed Mr. McGuire's face. "I have to meet someone," he said. "I won't be able to spend time with you."

"That doesn't matter," his wife answered, not easily discouraged. "Ned will spend the day with us. Then he can take the evening train back to St. John's."

"That way," Ned put in, "I'll be able to tell my father the big news."

"True," Mr. McGuire said. "I'll have my final answer today."

David and Anne were too busy quarrelling to hear the conversation, but Mary Lou had sharp ears. What did the conversation mean? Whatever it was, it was certainly not meant for her ears.

The day had risen dull and grey. The wind made hollows in the sea and the deep waves arched and rolled. The thought of a trip on the *Glencoe* worried Mary Lou. Not that she was afraid; she only hoped her father would not change his mind at the last minute.

"Maybe we shouldn't all go," Mr. McGuire said. "But I don't have a choice. I have to meet that government official."

But his wife would have none of it. "You need us," she protested.

He gave in, but did not look any less worried. His wife was right. It would be a comfort to have his family by his side on a day that would change their lives.

Despite the rough seas, the journey took place without incident. It was a pleasure to ride over the waves as the wind blew up trails of foam. Mary Lou refused to admit that the roll of the *Glencoe* made her seasick. She learned to keep her eyes on the horizon, which was the only stable point in this moving, rolling world. "I'm no greenhorn," she reminded herself. "After all, this isn't my first trip!"

Mary Lou was very glad to see the beautiful little port of Placentia come into view.

Overlooking a lagoon, the city was built on a flat, sandy peninsula formed by the silt of countless tides. Two long arms of water, eight and sixteen kilometres respectively, cut into the land. The Newfoundland-style houses introduced by the English along the Atlantic coast had replaced the French houses, though the French were the first to have colonized Placentia Bay. All along the coastline, they had left names of settlements that recalled the past: Cap Sainte-Marie, Brûlé, Crève-coeur, even Oderin.

Mr. McGuire went off to see a fellow magistrate and a government representative who was passing through the region.

“Good luck,” said Mrs. McGuire in a trembling voice. “Whatever you decide, it’ll be fine.”

As he strode away, his wife impatiently wiped away a tear.

Then she turned to her children. “Come now, everyone,” she said with authority. She herded the children from one part of town to the next. The streets were laid out at right angles, and at the end of each one was the sea. They passed an Anglican church, simple and handsome in style. The tombstones had almost all fallen over, and their inscriptions were all but worn away by time.

“Women sure died young back then!” Anne said indignantly as she read the dates.

Ned nodded. Human misery never failed to stir him. *He wants everybody to be happy*, Mary Lou thought, *but how can that be*?

Behind Placentia, the mountains rose up steep and dark. Mrs. McGuire pointed out the highest peak.

“That’s Castle Hill. We’ll go there this afternoon.”

They went to have lunch at the home of an old lady who turned out to be a cousin of theirs. It was amazing the way they had family everywhere in Newfoundland.

A little ferry took the band of explorers to the foot of Castle Hill and the train station. Mary Lou was no stranger to the railway, with its dark-red cars and steam locomotive.

Suddenly, from the direction of the station, they heard a dog barking. Mary Lou would have recognized that voice anywhere.

“Pierrot, oh, Pierrot!” she called out, breaking away from her family.

Who could mistake that massive frame covered in black

fleece, and that powerful body ready to make a playful leap? That was *her* dog tied up to a chain on the station platform. Pierrot planted his enormous paws on her shoulders, and the two friends tumbled to the ground. Mary Lou kneeled and threw her arms around Pierrot's strong body and buried her face in his woolly fur. Around the dog's neck was a label, just like for a package. The ship's owner certainly did things right.

Pierrot's bushy tail swept the ground like the pendulum of a clock. If dogs could smile, that's what Pierrot was doing as he barked a welcome for everyone.

David and Ned came running, and Pierrot greeted them, too. He was panting and as happy as a dog could be, but he still had plenty to say to Mary Lou, who was laughing and crying at the same time.

The station master, roused by the commotion, made an appearance. Although it was not really necessary, Mrs. McGuire told him, "This is our dog, sir."

The station master seemed cheered by the news. After all, what would he have done with Pierrot until the *Glencoe* departed for Oderin?

With Pierrot leading the way, pulling on his chain and Mary Lou at the same time, they began to climb Castle Hill. The pathway was bordered with wildflowers. Their progress was slow because of Jerome's short legs, so Mary Lou had to ask Pierrot to be patient.

"He's following the footsteps of Pierre Lemoine d'Iberville," said Ned.

Mary Lou did not like to be teased, but she could smell a good story. Ned was bit of a show-off with his knowledge, but she didn't care, because he loved his country and knew so much about it. D'Iberville was one of his favourite heroes who was still very much respected in Newfoundland. Only a bold man would have tried to take St. John's away from the English. And he had attacked by land.

"That would be the only way," Mary Lou said. "No one could get through that bottleneck harbour."

Starting out from Placentia on the first of November with four hundred men, he had travelled along the southern coast on snowshoes, partly through the woods, partly on the frozen waters of the bay.

"One hundred and twenty-eight kilometres on foot. Think of it!" said Ned enthusiastically.

It was hard to imagine. The same trip – even by train – had seemed endless to Mary Lou.

"No one was expecting them to come from that direction," Ned added. "On the way, they attacked Ferryland, Bay Bulls, Petty Harbour and St. John's."

"The only problem," David put in, "was that the French had already turned over their claims to Newfoundland to the English in 1713, after the treaty of Utrecht."

Suddenly they came out on the summit. But there was no fort there. Nothing remained but a few hillocks.

Ned explained, "This was once a star-shaped fort. Vauban, a French engineer who lived in the seventeenth century, designed it."

The fort was well situated, since it overlooked the passage to the sea, with Placentia spread out below it like a map. The landscape was glorious. It took your breath away – and not just because of the steep climb. The two arms of the sea that surrounded the city and its sandy beach looked more like twin rivers. Once the coast had belonged to France, part of the immense colonial empire that had stretched from Labrador to Louisiana.

The ocean breeze whipped up the waves and tangled Mary Lou's hair, and they had to take shelter behind the rocks to have their picnic. Ned continued with the story of Pierre Lemoine d'Iberville's career. He did not bear a grudge against him for having once done battle with the English; he respected the man's bravery.

"Those Frenchmen were rough fellows. They set up villages all down the Avalon coast. From Trinity Bay to Placentia, they laid a towpath for transporting fishing bait and even towing boats."

"How long was it?"

"Almost three thousand metres. They even thought of digging a canal between Bay Bulls and Come-by-Chance, so the sailing ships would not have to tack around the peninsula, which was dangerous."

Pierrot leaped to his feet with a shudder, then let loose a howl that sent echoes rolling down the hillside.

"Look, it's Papa!" Mary Lou called out.

Mr. McGuire was too out of breath to talk. In his frenetic affection, Pierrot put his big paws on Mr. McGuire's shoulders and licked his cheeks.

"Saved in the nick of time!" he burst out after Mary Lou grabbed hold of Pierrot's collar.

Mrs. McGuire and the children crowded around him. By her husband's calm expression, she could tell the matter was settled.

"I have big news for us," he announced. "Come autumn, we'll be living in St. John's!"

"Living in St. John's!"

Mary Lou was stunned. So *that* was the mystery that had preoccupied her parents for all these months! She

Mrs. McGuire and the children crowded around him.

remembered their secretive words and strange references, and all those mysterious plans.

"We're finally leaving Oderin," David said, half to himself.

Anne saw the consequences right away. "That means we won't be going to boarding school!"

"That's one big reason for moving," her father said. "And I've been offered a job in St. John's as well." Silencing the uproar, he added, "We're going back to Oderin tonight. We'll be leaving in an hour with the tide."

Mr. McGuire started down towards the town, but then he turned and retraced his steps. He put his arm around Mary Lou's shoulders and gently led her down the path. He understood his daughter and her wild heart, and he loved Oderin as much as she did. In a way, they would always be exiles from their native island.

At the government dock, the schooner moved to and fro, shaken by mysterious currents that spoke of a coming storm. In the distance, iron-grey clouds were piling up. The children were not afraid, but Mr. McGuire could read the sea's intentions almost as well as the sailors could.

"I think we should have left earlier," he said. "The weather's not bad yet, but I'm expecting the worst."

"Let's wait till tomorrow," Mrs. McGuire suggested.

"We can stay at our cousin's," Anne put in.

David burst out laughing, "Can you picture all of us showing up with Pierrot?"

"No," Mr. McGuire decided. "If we stay on, the storm might keep us here for days." And in the meantime, he knew, someone might need his services in Oderin. For a little while longer, the islanders were still his family.

CHAPTER THIRTEEN

Caught in the Storm

THE CLOUDS PILED UP, THE WIND BLEW, AND gusts tore foam from the sea. Mary Lou held down her skirt with one hand and her scarf with the other. Her cheeks were stung by the wind-borne spray, but she smiled. She enjoyed the storm. Instead of frightening her, it made her feel alive. With searching eyes, David stood at the bow of the schooner, watching for Oderin on the horizon.

But Jerome was afraid, and her parents could not hide their concern, either. Pierrot, who had bedded down in a corner among the ropes, sniffed the salty air and gave a low growl. The ship was tossed about. It squeaked, cracked and plunged deep between the crests of the waves, protesting all the while.

Finally they reached Oderin and stopped away from the shore. The landing boats pulled on their cords, tossed by the rising storm. The captain called out orders, and the sailors dropped anchor and lowered two dories into the water. Rowers settled into the little boats to carry the passengers to shore.

Placentia Bay could be dangerous at times, and Phillip McGuire wished he had not been so eager to leave. With furrowed brow, Mrs. McGuire tried to make her voice sound reassuring. The children thought it was all a grand adventure. Crouching low in the boats, they nestled under large oilcloths that protected them from the spray. Pierrot turned this way and that and put everyone in danger, but Mary Lou managed to calm him down.

They beached on the sandy shore and all breathed a sigh of relief. Dozens of pairs of eyes watched them, for all of Oderin had gathered along the harbour.

"What a great storm," Mary Lou said, enjoying herself.

But the looks she got made her squirm.

"Two fishing dories haven't gotten back yet," David whispered to her.

Then she spotted Brigitte, whose face was tormented by worry. Her mother had had to stay at home with little Martha, and Brigitte had been sent out to bring back word. Mary Lou saw two women with faces frozen like tragic masks: Tom's mother and aunt. Tom himself was standing at the end of the wharf. Leaning against the wind, he was as motionless as a statue.

Then he turned and cupped his hands around his mouth. "There's a dory out there!"

The minutes stretched on forever, as the islanders' hearts ticked off the endless seconds. Tom's whole being was tense with effort, and he kept his eyes peeled, as though his very will would make his father come into view. But then his shoulders slumped and his hands dropped wearily to his sides.

His mother understood. It wasn't her husband's boat. His aunt stifled a sob, for her husband and son Ben had sailed with Thomas Griffith, as they did every day, and they were out there, too.

Brigitte ran down the wharf. Her father was the lucky one who had made it back. Beaten down, soaked to the skin, the life gone from his eyes, Mr. Jarvis did not have the strength to tell what a fight it had been to get home.

Night came on and the group dispersed. Only Mr. McGuire kept a vigil with Tom and his family. The wind howled, the storm raged twice as angrily, and the sea sang a magnificent, wild dirge. Mary Lou would never talk about enjoying a storm again. If it was so hard for a big schooner to sail in weather like this, what would become of a little dory?

The waves came crashing up to the houses, and the islanders barricaded their doors and windows. For a split second, lightning sent its zigzagging arrows to illuminate the black sky. Above the hills, thunder growled like a beast. People gathered around candles to pray aloud, and the light danced on their faces.

Hours later, a terrible piece of news made the rounds. The Griffith dory had crashed on the reefs. Everyone rushed down to the beach. There in the tumult of unchained natural fury, people stood, mute with fear.

Pieces of wood were strewn over the black rocks. Across the bay from the wharf, on Seagull Rock, three men were hanging onto a ledge being beaten by the dark waves. The ledge was too narrow to get much footing on, and the fishermen were clinging desperately to it.

They had to be rescued! Tom rushed forward, pushing the new dory he had only just finished.

It took the waves only a few seconds to overturn the fragile craft. The same fate befell the other boats that the determined fishermen dragged into the water. Not a single dory got farther than the first foamy whirlpools. Pulling their capsized boats, the men came swimming back, and stood helplessly trying to see out to the rock through the rain and wind. A new day came and went by. Then another night. The storm raged on.

Finally, after forty-eight hours, the sea grew calm. Seagull Rock stood like a dark mass against the sky.

Tom was the first to set out. The dory he was so proud of made its maiden voyage. Others followed in pursuit. Soon there was an entire flotilla of green, yellow and white hulls stretching out like a brightly coloured bouquet.

Tom returned with his cousin. He was the only one of the three men who still remained clinging to Seagull Rock when the storm ended. Ben was lying on the bottom of the dory, moaning and unconscious. He was quickly taken to the McGuire house, where the injured and sick of Oderin were cared for. Could Phillip and Isabelle McGuire bring him back to life?

The people of Oderin returned to their homes, to wait for the news anxiously.

One man remained at the spot: Angus MacDonald. Facing the sea, he thought of the misfortune that had shaped his own life. The sea . . . he bore a grudge against her yet she gave him his living. He respected her, he dreaded her, yet he would not have chosen any other way.

He was lost in his thoughts when suddenly he heard an unexpected sound. Was that a sob he heard? He walked towards a clump of bushes where the sound came from. Pushing aside the branches, he saw Mary Lou, looking tiny and frail, huddling against Pierrot.

"This is nothing for a little girl to see," he muttered in a gruff voice. Then he gathered her up in his arms and gently brushed aside her tears.

"Be strong now, for the others," he said.

He quickly set off for her house. Clinging to him, she felt something cold and hard under his shirt: a stick of dynamite! But this time she forgot to be afraid. Instead, she listened to his low, comforting words. It sounded as though he were talking to himself.

The McGuire house was full of people. Ben had been laid on the couch in the hospital room. For two days, the island held its breath as Ben fought for his life in the narrow room. Then, thanks to his strength and youth, he finally woke up.

It happened during Mary Lou's watch. When Ben sat up suddenly, it startled her. His eyes were marked with dark circles, his skin was white as paper, his beard was shaggy, and his lips trembled. He stared at a point just beyond Mary Lou and pointed his finger towards the door. *He's imagining things*, she thought.

In a broken voice, he uttered, "The dog! There, I see him."

She was relieved and burst out laughing. "Of course. It's Pierrot. He followed me in."

"That can't be. I sold him. He left. He's not here anymore."

Then she understood. Ben was the one who had taken her dog, and his cousin Tom had known it all along! But how could she be angry when Ben was so sick and miserable?

A little later, she sat down next to her father. He was on the porch, writing letters. There were so many things to take care of before the autumn.

The clear blue sky arched over the island like a dome. Lazy waves washed against the shores. How could such a friendly world hold those storms? It was hard to believe, yet Mary Lou had seen nature's violence with her own eyes.

"What are you thinking about?" asked her father, drawing her near.

When she told him of her discovery, he advised her to

keep the secret. "No one must know about Ben's confession. Even Tom should think we don't know the truth. It's better that way."

"I promise I won't say a thing."

Ben grew stronger every day. That same week, he and Tom took to the sea together for the first time. At the end of the afternoon, David stood on the wharf, enviously awaiting their return. He spotted their dory in the distance. Its lines were elegant and its yellow hull was already stained with salt. How well the boat sailed! It looked balanced and easy to steer. The way it sat low in the water meant the catch had been good.

Ben and Tom jumped onto the beach, and Ben got busy dragging in the nets. Tom lingered a moment, discussing the day's work. He had changed now, too: he had become a true fisherman. His life depended on his strength and judgement. He was a man now.

Compared to him, David was still a boy. For years to come, he would continue studying, readying himself for the adult world. Meanwhile, Tom was already part of it. As Tom himself had predicted, their paths were separating. But did their separation have to be bitter?

David had promised himself he would not lose this old friendship. Silently he helped Tom and Ben carry in the fish.

CHAPTER FOURTEEN
Clearing the Decks

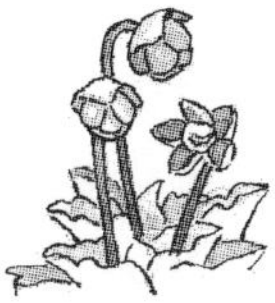

LIKE THE YEAR BEFORE, DAVID'S DEPARTURE marked the beginning of autumn. The *Glencoe* would be casting off that night, and David intended to use the remaining hours to the fullest.

Mr. McGuire was taking photographs of the big house that soon would no longer be their home. The camera he had received at Christmas had not been used much so far. The first pictures it would take would be the last ones of Oderin.

He spotted David and Mary Lou running a race. David was far ahead of his sister, but Pierrot outdistanced them both.

"Come over here and I'll take your picture in front of the house!"

The children were glad to oblige, but it turned out to be more than they had bargained for. Their father was both a beginner and a perfectionist. He adjusted the lens a dozen times, moved up, stepped back, hesitated, then started over. Finally he lost patience. His models were moving around too much, especially Pierrot, who was rhythmically beating the ground with his tail.

"Papa, do you want me to take over?"

David's comment earned him a dressing-down. Mr. McGuire knew nothing about photography, but he intended to be up to date and understand these modern inventions. He would figure things out for himself without asking his son for help.

Once the pictures had been taken, David and Mary Lou decided to go on a long walk. They climbed the island's highest hill, at its northernmost point, where a river cascaded down a cliff. As they neared it, every other sound melted into its continuous, seething roar.

Pierrot, who had followed them, lapped at the rushing water. At this height on the island, the trees did not reach their normal size. They sent their roots down into the scanty ground to drop anchor among the rocks underneath. From the scrawny trees hung tender green garlands, strange-looking mushrooms that the islanders called old man's beards.

David and Mary Lou pushed aside the bushes and discovered plants that grew in abundance in the humid places in this northern climate. A few dried berries still hung from their stems; they were the fruit of the anis plant, dull and white, like tiny eggs. At the beginning of the season, their pleasant smell and taste of wintergreen made them a favourite food. There were still a few crackerberries left. Their wild-cherry taste made them a delicacy, and David and Mary Lou devoured handfuls of them, until soon their tongues were red and pulpy.

They sat down on the rocks that overlooked the scene. The cold air was refreshing and the tiny drops from the cascading waters washed their faces. Soon they would be leaving the island of their birth. But its beauty would remain, even if they moved on.

"This waterfall was here long before any man lived on this continent," David said.

"You think so?"

With David as teacher, geography lessons did not seem so hard. He told Mary Lou of the beginnings of Newfoundland, the true beginnings, back when the land really was new.

He pulled his watch from his pocket and dangled it over the river canyon. Hanging from its silver chain, the watch swung left, then right, as regular as a pendulum, hypnotizing. The Roman numerals stood out in black, like insect feet on the flat face. Skittish, the second hand made one sweep, then another, then started a third.

David sighed. Another two hours and he would be going into exile again to boarding school, and leaving Oderin forever. When vacation came again, he would not be returning here.

"We'd better get home," he said, standing up.

When he and Mary Lou climbed down to the narrow road, they were really bidding farewell to their charmed childhood, so free and wild.

With David gone, the house seemed deserted. The days were endless, especially now that the school was closed. Mary Lou missed the call of the bell, the mad rush with her books under her arm to make it in time, the laughter and games during recess, and even Mr. Burke's commanding voice.

Mrs. McGuire knew her daughter was sad, which was why she found countless errands for Mary Lou to do. The jobs she was given were meant to make her forget her dark thoughts.

Mrs. McGuire loved the autumn. It was a busy time for her, as she readied the house for winter. In Oderin, a little community that depended solely on its own resources, everything had to be thought out in advance. You could not afford to make any mistakes. But this year, Mary

Lou did not like what she saw. Unlike past years, the family was not storing up tons of provisions, but only enough to live on until their November departure.

At least they had time to pick the roses and admire them. They were more beautiful than ever, because they would be the last ones from Oderin. The food the McGuires had stored was distributed across the island: to Tom's family, now that the head of the house was gone, and to Brigitte's, which had the added responsibility of little Martha.

It was almost as if Christmas were not going to happen this year. There was no mysterious correspondence with the St. John's shopkeepers, and no Christmas cake to fill the big kitchen with the delicious smell of spices and raisins. Jams were made, though not very many, just gooseberry and blueberry. That way, they could take a little of Oderin with them.

The family did not give up its annual expedition to Cape Roger, known for its wild berries, but they went for the fun. The McGuires set out for the cape on a clear, cool day. The translucent, amber blackberries looked like little pearls in the hollows of their rounded leaves. The rosy-cheeked pickers looked a little like berries themselves, with their eyes sparkling in the cold and their big sailors' sweaters up to their ears. The sharp, acid smell of the fruit mingled with the scent of the sea, iodine and salt together. The next day, they would spread out the harvest on the table to sort it. The spoiled fruit would be set aside, and the rest would be preserved with plenty of sugar. Later, in St. John's, they would remember this day.

In mid-October, they decided to pack up the attic. It had always been off-limits to the children, though they had snuck into it once or twice on the sly, with beating hearts. This time, they marched in with their mother.

The attic was immense. Uncle Paul's house in St. John's would have easily fit inside, and you could have thrown in the garden, too, for good measure.

She climbed aboard and soon was pushing off with all her might ...

The lamp threw a pool of light around them, making the leather of the open-mouthed trunks glow. Mrs. McGuire dove into one of them and began her task. Anne, already an excellent worker, helped her.

Meanwhile, Mary Lou spotted a swing that David had hung from the ceiling. She climbed aboard and soon was pushing off with all her might, soaring towards the attic window, a triangle of grey sky.

When she was younger, she used to dream of a land called Somewhere Else. She had built that country with her own imagination after Anne, at her wits' end, had told her noisy sister, "Go play somewhere else."

Somewhere Else, Somewhere Else. . . . The country was like a coloured dot on the sea on some imaginary map. Were its mysterious inhabitants called "Else-ese" like the Portuguese, "Else-iards" like the Spaniards, or "Else-ians" like the Brazilians? In the rafters, Mary Lou was back in that world. She was swinging away, humming a tune.

Months later, in the spring – the McGuires' first spring in St. John's – her father hung the same swing from a tree in the yard. All Mary Lou had to do was close her eyes, and she could smell the scent of the musty attic and feel the atmosphere of the house on Oderin.

CHAPTER FIFTEEN

The Pathway to the Future

THE *GLENCOE* DROPPED ANCHOR IN ODERIN ON the 31st of October. Among the passengers was Father Cox. He had come from his parish in Burin to celebrate All Saints' Day with the islanders.

But where would Father Cox stay? The McGuires were leaving the next day, and everything was packed, including the extra beds, sheets and blankets.

"This house has never refused hospitality to a priest, and the last day will be no exception," Mrs. McGuire decreed.

Father Cox, who had seen rougher times, was happy with very little. He had come to baptize the youngest members of Oderin's society. The babies took centre stage. Mr. McGuire went to get the black box lined with satin. From it, Father Cox took a white cloth, a candle and a crucifix.

All four future recipients of baptism were impatient. The smallest was only eight days old, while the oldest, Brigitte's sister, was three months. Mary Lou became Martha's godmother, with Mr. McGuire standing as godfather. In the name of her goddaughter, Mary Lou recited the prescribed formulas in a steady voice.

Then came the visits to the sick. With Mr. McGuire holding the lamp, Father Cox strode along the deserted roads. He took advantage of the opportunity to speak of David.

"I saw David at school," the priest said. "He's a solid chap."

"Yes," his father answered. "He's more serious than he used to be."

Silence settled in. Then the priest cleared his throat.

"David asked me to speak of his plans. He wants to become a missionary."

Mr. McGuire's hand trembled, and the pool of lantern-light swung and shimmered in the night. He had been willing to be separated from his son so he could study. Now, going to live in St. John's meant they would be closer. And just as they were about to be together again, was David going to go off to some foreign country for years, perhaps for life? Why had he not told his father the news first? For a boy to become a man, Mr. McGuire realized, perhaps he has to break away from his parents when it comes time to make decisions.

After a long silence, Mr. McGuire said, "I'll write to say I'm proud of him."

On their last day in Oderin, they rose early. All their friends had gathered in the brightly lit little church. The candles burned, songs of elation rose into the air, and the day of all saints was celebrated. It was a solemn, magnificent farewell to the island shrouded in morning mist.

Mary Lou ran down to the beach where the *Glencoe* was waiting. In a few hours, it would carry the McGuires to St. John's, bag and baggage. Pierrot would be on board, too. The dog scampered around Mary Lou, wondering why she was acting so strangely. What was going to happen this morning? Some sort of madness was sweeping the entire family. Mary Lou felt like crying as she shook Ben Griffith's hand. Taciturn, already carrying the load of a hard life, Ben had come down to wish her a good trip.

But Tom was her one true companion. He stood before her with a serious look on his face.

"Oh, Tom, I don't want to leave you, I don't want to leave any of you!"

"You have to, Mary Lou. Besides, your heart has already left us. Soon I'll be going, too. I'll be a captain of an ocean-going ship, and I'll come and see you as often as I can."

"Do you think we can be happy away from Oderin?"

"You can, Mary Lou. You're not a little girl anymore."

At last the boat pulled away. Mary Lou watched her friends wave to her from the wharf. Tom was with Ben. Apart from the others stood Angus MacDonald, smoking his pipe. Brigitte had insisted on bringing little Martha with her. The baby was howling, obviously a sign that she was glad to be alive. In her, a small part of Mary Lou would remain on the island.

Pierrot was pacing the bridge. After all his voyages, he had earned his sea legs. He frisked here and there, drawn by the intoxicating scent of the ropes, the seaweed and the oil. Soon he brought her mind around to other thoughts.

Pierrot ran free on Oderin. Would he get used to the narrow streets and hundreds of people all jammed together in the same place? Would he be able to sort out the smells that would assault his nose? Would he be unhappy in the city?

The island, her island, grew distant, prey to the winds that swept its surface. Shaken by the waves, the boat headed for the Newfoundland coast. With its hard hand, the wind caressed Mary Lou's long hair. She felt uprooted as she leaned against the rail, watching the swelling waves.

How cold the air suddenly felt on this early November day!

In the city, Mary Lou would never feel this close to the seasons. She felt them in her bones, in her heart. She was attached to the sea by every sinew in her body, like the trees that clung to the rocks of Oderin.

Mary Lou turned to her mother. Normally light-hearted, Mrs. McGuire was staring off into the distance. Two tears rolled down her cheeks. Mr. McGuire put his arm around his wife's shoulders. He spoke to her gently, then beckoned Mary Lou to his side.

Escorted by Pierrot, who always made her feel braver, she went to him. Thanks to the sea, they had the world at their doorstep. And now that Mary Lou was on the threshold of a new life, she did not need to look back to Oderin. She carried the island within her just as surely as her own heart.

For Oderin was a stepping-stone to the future.

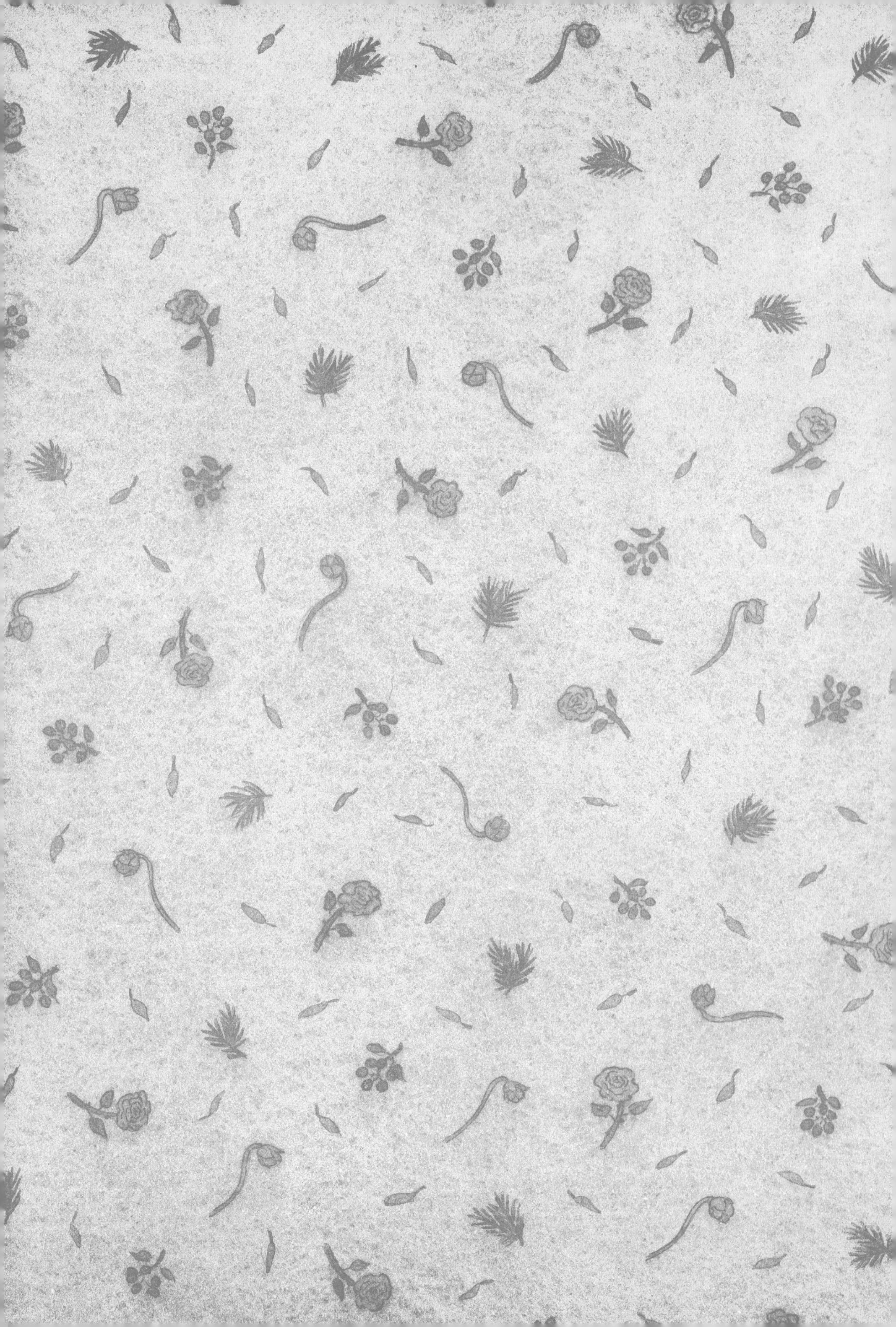